Being Home

An Anthology

Being Home

An Anthology

Edited by Sam Pickering
& Bob Kunzinger

Lake Dallas, Texas

Table of Contents

Introductory Notes

Sam Pickering

Words make homes, not bricks and mortar, not even furnishings and family. As words change so do homes. Nowadays I live in an old person's home. It was a different place when I bought it forty years ago. Since then the stairs have gotten steeper. Liver spots have appeared on walls, and cracks wrinkle across ceilings. The living and dining rooms have aged into storerooms piled high with boxes. Once I knew their contents. Now I don't know or care. Upstairs closets are thick with clothes worn by me's that have disappeared. At first three children shared the home with Vicki and me. Time passed, and they grew up and left. Now three small rescue dogs are our family. All are over fifteen years old and two suffer from canine senility.

Years ago, I read to learn more than for entertainment. I still read for entertainment, but now more for recollection. As I turn pages, I discover who I was, where I have been, and sometimes where I am going, or not going. Memory is a wizard. It changes nonfiction into fiction, and fiction into nonfiction. As I read the pieces in this anthology not only fragments from the lives I led and might have led came to mind, but I also wandered the homes the authors described. I wasn't comfortable in all the homes, but I experienced them. Like the Seven-league Boots of Little Poucet and the Magical Carpets of Isfahan, reading transformed my armchair and teacake existence, and I traveled to worlds simultaneously familiar and different, new and old.

Strangers ask contributors to this anthology where they are from, a question that no one can answer to his own satisfaction. Other contributors discover they are "not from around here," no matter how long they've been in the neighborhood. A person lives in an Accident House. On the street outside cars crash, inside people bruise one another. Some contributors discover they cannot go home, but, of course, in their pieces they return to a home. How does a person fashion a home in a distant land, and when she leaves, does that home vanish into the mist of years? A woman is at home in the history of the Holocaust. A man researches his family. He fails to discover his ancestry, but in the process what he learns about others becomes his facts. For some narrators, and readers, books make a home. A man takes imaginary walks through Chicago to keep close to the boy he "once was and to the family" he came from. I accompanied him; it was my first visit to Chicago. After a fifty-two-year absence, a man visits the village once home to the small school in Connecticut he attended. I went with him part of the way, but then I drifted northeast to Maine and later south to Tennessee.

"Place is the anchor; the rich soil in which we take root," a woman writes. For some writers the soil is rich; for others it's barren till. For many readers, place mesmerizes. Several writers cultivate gardens, and their homes bloom. For a woman and her husband home is forty years of hiking. A woman who misses the open landscape of Montana looks out a window and studies the close hills of New Hampshire so that "what might be can take root." A couple remembers housemates who left indelible prints on their lives. In their pieces, writers mark passings. As a boy, one narrator lived in many houses. Before leaving he helped his father paint the walls. In each wall, he left behind a single pin hole. What does anyone leave behind? Certainly, it is always a pinhole, but if it is accessible like the pieces in this anthology, readers can look through it and see richness in themselves and without and see it in poverty and unhappiness as well as pleasure and joy. For untold moments they will live both their lives and the lives of the narrators. Perhaps they'll sit and wander Never-Never Lands, in the process creating homes with words. In the beginning and in the middle and at the end are words.

So, where are you from?

Bob Kunzinger

When someone asks the standard question, "Where is home for you?" at a conference, a ballgame, or an airport, or anywhere we go really and meet someone new, the answer for many is not so easy. "Well, I live in Virginia, but I'm from New York," or some variation of those two realities—where we live and where we grew up—is typical. Rarely do we meet people anymore who have lived in one spot their entire lives. We have to go to Europe for that, the "old country," where ancestry drills deep into centuries past, rarely wandering more than a few hundred kilometers from one spot.

But the concept of "home" is complicated in our transient, emigrating world. For my part, I usually say New York, though I suppose I could say Ireland, or Germany, or Italy if I had my DNA chart with me. I could even suggest my roots return to the Celtic nomads of five thousand years ago though it is hard for me to pinpoint where, to be certain. Instead I say New York. I have lived in Virginia for well more than half my life and my current house in a small village for twenty-four years, but I am a "come lately" here. And my native neighbors are correct; I will never be "from" Virginia. My son is, though, born and raised here.

The essays in this collection explore that fluid definition of home. These revealing works wander from the notion that "home is where your stuff is," as George Carlin asserted, to home is where your family is, whether it be a Brooklyn brownstone, a 3B 2 ½ B suburban 2 car garage ranch, or an automobile. One motif is decidedly consistent herein: "Where is home?" is more often answered in reference to a person's genetic code than a zip code.

Excellent writing reaches up and out of itself; it shows us our pain and often unearths treasured memories and tribulations we thought we had buried for good. With those guidelines, these works invite us not simply into the writers' homes—ancestral and contemporary—but into our own as well.

Ignorance or Innocence

Johnnie Bernhard

I had to leave. It was not my home. It was my father's home. He moved us from the suburbs of Houston to the flat coastal plains of South Texas in 1974. Forty years later, I remember the two extremes as visions: the Houston skyline shadowed by petrochemical plants with thermal flares lighting the night like shooting stars, and Ganado, tired and gray, with one road cutting through town and a blinking caution light swinging in the wind. Life was just like that then, one extreme to another.

The people I went to school with were mostly farmers' children or the working poor, Whites, Blacks, and Mexicans, with too many children and too many bills. They rode bulls and quarter horses in rodeos, drove combines that harvested corn, worked for a local merchant for $1.75 an hour, or were migrant farm workers, who lived at a nondescript motel at the edge of town.

They were proud people, said what was on their mind, and moved without hesitation. They loved and hated the same way, unencumbered. With little restraint in their actions, they *drank* hard and they *worked* hard. It was either ignorance or innocence that motivated them. The farm to market roads of South Texas were littered with beer cans, punctured spleens, and twisted limbs every weekend as a testimony to their creed.

On Monday morning, we huddled in our desks in home room, anticipating the news of a classmate propelled through a windshield into a barbed wired fence. For years, a blonde, chocolate-eyed cheerleader, whose head was severed in a car accident, has haunted my middle-aged dreams. She never ages, forever sixteen and beautiful.

My best friend and her family lived in a two-bedroom house that hadn't seen a coat of paint in thirty years. They were Bohemians, not in the artistic sense, but part of an ethnic group of Czechs who arrived in Texas in the late nineteenth century. In the pecking order of a small Texas town, they were slightly above Blacks and Mexicans. Poor, Catholic, and of eastern European descent, this family was handed a first-class ticket to the edge of town; a place where they rented from a prominent family until some miracle came along.

Five children slept in one bedroom and the parents in the other. There was no central air or heat. In the winter, a twenty-five-inch-wide gas heater provided heat for seven people. The trick was to sequentially move your front and back sides in the middle of those twenty-five inches of heat, ensuring even distribution of warmth. This was not easily done in a large family; arguments and shoving were part of the morning ritual.

"Don't stand so close to that damn thing! You'll catch your night gown on fire!" I did stand too close. And in return for my disobedience, I received second degree burns on the back of my calves resembling grill marks on a steak.

The only happy day I remember in that family's life was the day the miracle arrived. They moved into their own home. The man who sold it to them had been their former landlord. The house needed a lot of work, but it had three bedrooms. The only son had a room of his own when he was sixteen. The four daughters shared a room.

My father helped sheet-rock and paint that house in exchange of my friend's father pouring a concrete sidewalk in front of our house. The two men tried to forge a friendship with whiskey and labor, but it didn't last.

The last time I saw my friend was a year after high school graduation. I received a small college scholarship and left town the morning after graduation. She stayed and got married. When I returned home for summer break, I went by her house, her home as a married woman. She showed me her photo album of the wedding shower and wedding. The highlight was the prenuptial shower where the hostesses presented the bride to be with a penis-shaped cake. The photograph showed women posing around the cake with their arms draped on each other's shoulders. There was a comradery there I recognized immediately, as one who did not belong.

I never saw her again after that. I can't remember why. The only news that came over the years was that her father tried to commit suicide in the only home he ever owned.

A lot of girls became pregnant during that four-year trial known as high school. Someone explained it to me as, "Only the good girls get caught." At the time, I remember being confused by the word "caught" and what it had to do with being good.

During my sophomore year, a girl a year older than me went into labor in the high school bathroom. I didn't know she was pregnant. I didn't know if she was a good girl. The only thing I knew about her was she wore her father's shirts to school, and she hated to read. Once in civics class the teacher asked her to read out loud. She immediately put her head on her desk and covered it with both arms, becoming invisible in the enormity of her father's white shirt.

During that same time, I hosted a baby shower for a pregnant sixteen-year-old girl. Five girls came to the shower I gave in the living room. The mother of the pregnant teen refused to come. The one family member to attend was an older sister, who sat on the couch, unsmiling, clutching her purse in her lap, poised for flight at any minute.

By hosting the baby shower, I forever labeled myself as an outsider. I wasn't from there. I never would be one of them. It was the same for my mother. She knew it at the time and didn't care. It took me longer to figure it out, because I accepted their excuses. "I can't come to your party, because I'm sick." "I can't come to your party, because we're going out of town." "I can't come to your party, because my mother thinks you're white trash."

There was plenty of ostracizing to go around, but it was always worse for the girls who became pregnant in high school. The social norms of a small Texas town in the Seventies sent pregnant, unwed mothers to live with a distant relative or a church home with the simple, direct marquee, *Texas Home for Unwed Mothers.*

The irony of the town's moral code was cruel: if you plan for sex, you're a slut, but don't get pregnant and embarrass us. No one knew that cruelty more than the pregnant, unwed mother. As soon as her belly swelled, she was gone, sent away with no forwarding address left behind. No one talked about it.

Sometimes the girl would return with her baby. But

she was different. Her sadness pervaded the entire school building. She was no longer a schoolgirl, but a mother with a broken heart.

The guest of honor at the baby shower in my mother's living room kept her baby and married the baby's father. That violent boy became a violent man until he was killed on an offshore oil rig. The young widow with two children remained in the trailer house he bought for her.

My mother felt sorry for that girl, like she did for a lot of the disenfranchised of that little town. I suppose most of her life she felt the same way, but she refused to accept it as a life sentence. She was one of the town's eccentrics—a black-headed, red-lipstick-wearing Catholic from South Louisiana. She was too much for that little town— too soulful, too emotional, too rice and gravy Cajun. The Protestant, gentry farmers of German descent in Ganado didn't like her. A lot of people thought she was crazy.

There were a lot of stories about my mom in those days. One remains with me. When my eight-year-old sister refused to wear the new shoes my mother bought her, my mother was outraged. Without a word, she quickly packed my sister's shoes and clothes and stuffed them into paper grocery bags. With the clothes in the trunk of her car and her four daughters in the back seat of the yellow 1976 Oldsmobile 98 Regency, my mother drove to the motel near Highway 59.

The motel was a cinder block building of once white drabness, plopped on a concrete pad without a single plant, tree, or weed in its wake. It was a stopping point for truck drivers traveling Highway 59, and the seasonal home of the migrant farm workers and their children.

My mother walked inside the motel office, only turning

around once, silently forbidding us from getting out of the car. When she came out of the motel office a few minutes later, a man followed her. She handed him the paper bags of clothes with the pair of new shoes on top.

We didn't say a word on the ride home. We stared straight ahead in the heat of the South Texas sun; our bare legs sweating, sticking to the vinyl covered car seats.

I never thought my mother was crazy. I thought she was courageous. She hosted a baby shower for a girl the town was ashamed of and gave clothes to migrant farm workers everyone called wet backs.

Forty years later, I cannot separate two images of her: the picture of the little girl in her First Communion photograph clutching a white lily with white-gloved hands, and an expressionless middle-aged woman with black hair and red lips drinking coffee on the side porch of our house in Ganado.

My first job was in that little town. The owner's son rode his bicycle to the Dairy Mart every day. His dog Bobo rode in the wire basket near the handlebars. Society had many names for Rusty then: retard, mongoloid, idiot, and moron.

Our job was to close the restaurant. The first thing Rusty did after the last customer left was turn up the radio. He then stacked the dining room chairs, sometimes six chairs high. Together, we carried five-gallon buckets of hot water and vinegar for mopping the floor. We worked from the back to the entrance, pushing our mops across the linoleum floor of the dining room.

At the entrance door, we rested the mops outside the building. I reached back inside the dining room and turned off the light. Once the door was locked, Rusty would holler, "Good night!" and whistle for his dog sleeping near his bicycle. Off the two of them would ride, in the quiet, deserted streets of Ganado on a weekday night in the late Seventies.

I kept that job until I graduated from high school. I said goodbye to everyone beginning the morning of my graduation from school and Ganado.

I met my friends that morning on a farm outside of town, where we ceremoniously stripped to our bras and panties and swam in a rice canal. There, the irrigation pump bellowed clear, cold water into the lushness of early rice. It was the last time we were all together, laughing.

The next day I left the blinking caution light at the four way stop of Ganado, forever. What I brought with me was a realization that life was a chasm between ignorance and innocence. This made me a target, but also a runner. Every four way stop I came to in life, I encountered like I did that swinging caution light in Ganado. I plowed through it and never looked back. I ran and ran until my heart burst, and the small-town girl was completely lost somewhere along the way.

I returned to Ganado last summer to bury my father. My past came to the funeral service. It spoke to me as if everything were unchanged, despite the passing of thirty-three years. I was that girl who lived in the white house on the corner and worked at the Dairy Mart. I was still the girl "not from here."

Celibacy and Ancestry

Rick Campbell

Belonging,
After all, is mostly a matter of belief.
—Leslie Norris

The search for Baby Schaeffer—it all but worked out, but I couldn't let it be. I had him, but like Oedipus, I had to keep pushing, prying, asking one more question. I wanted to belong; I had to believe.

In the late 70s, as an undergrad, I began reading about American utopian societies and was surprised to see the Harmonists and Economy in my textbook. As a child I'd taken school field trips to Old Economy and though then I did not listen to a word that was said, when I came across it again, I read with fervor. The Harmonists lived under many names. George Rapp was the first and greatest leader. Rapp came from Germany, a radical, mystical Lutheran who was charismatic enough to have followers and dangerous enough to the powers that ruled Germany in 1800 to get him arrested and then to make his migration to the New World seem a good deal to him and his enemies. Rapp bought land in the hills of Western Pennsylvania and brought his followers there where they built a town called

Harmony. A few years later they moved to Indiana and started New Harmony. But that turned out to be not to their liking and they sold it to Robert Owen and moved back to settle on prime Ohio riverfront land. A brochure written by the Harmony Society museum calls this land primeval forest. Maybe so, but as I grew up there nothing seemed primeval, unless it was the steel mill's fire at night. This third, and last, settlement, they called Oekonomie (a place of orderly, managed affairs) which in English became Economy. These are the people I wanted to be descended from; these are who I wanted as family. Who would I be? A Rappite, A Harmonist? An Economite?

I wanted to belong to a group of people who had intentionally banded together for a good reason, even if it wasn't my reason. When I believed in God it wasn't their Protestant God. I'm also attracted to the contradiction in my title. Celibacy does not beget ancestry. They are, if everyone behaves by the rules, mutually exclusive terms. In every group, not everyone plays by the rules, and rumor had it that even George Rapp didn't always embrace celibacy. There was at least one sweet young Harmonist that caught his eye, and maybe more than just his eye. But Rapp and the Harmonist elders were not, like others, like the Oneida Perfectionists, horny old men who believed that young women needed to be initiated into sexual intercourse by the grizzled veterans of the Love Boat. By and large the Harmonist elders seemed to keep their promises and keep their pants zipped, or tied, or whatever they did in the early 1800s to keep their privates housed and holstered.

So how could I have any hope of being descended from these guys? Schism, that's how. The Harmony Society was cruising along in its third incarnation at Economy, a beautiful site downriver from Pittsburgh; they had over 500 members and were generally healthy, wealthy and wise. Then came the Lion of Judah. A French false prophet that Rapp and the other leaders embraced with open arms, the Lion claimed to be Count de Leon, but his real name was Bernhard (Mueller) Maximilian Proli, and what he was espousing more than anything else, was let's get it on. His song caught on with almost a third of the Economy faithful. Soon, a large contingent of followers who couldn't wait to resume connubial relations left the Society and headed a few more miles downriver to Phillipsburg. There, we might assume, they had lots of sex since they were willing to part ways with George Rapp, family and friends and to a large extent, crucial tenets of belief. This was a bit like the Civil War in the way family members supported both sides of the Sex vs Celibacy issue. However, there were also some guilt-ridden Germans when it came to dealing with sex and pleasure. One account of Harmonist backsliders talks of them groveling in front of Father Rapp, begging forgiveness for their sexual transgression and asking to be returned to the celibate flock. They seemed to suffer from a huge post coital depression after they gave in to their carnal desires.

It's hard to believe that a sober and probably level-headed leader like George Rapp would be taken in by a fake Count who, besides faking his royalty, also claimed to be the Messiah. It's clear to us now that he wasn't, or if he was, almost anyone can be the Messiah. Who really knows what the Messiah is supposed to do? Be a deliverer, a savior, but from what? Bernard saved his people from celibacy, maybe that counts too. Stranger still, Harmonist historians claim that Rapp was "expecting the Messiah in

1829." Rapp and his followers were Millennialists; they expected the kingdom of God to come in their time and they thought their time would come soon. Hence, their declaration of celibacy in 1807. But expecting the Messiah in 1829 is pretty specific. It's like Joe Namath (an indirect product of the Harmonist experiment) prophesying victory in the Super Bowl. Rapps's Harmonist followers were getting a little anxious and grumpy waiting for the end of the world and maybe that's why Rapp welcomed Bernhard Proli with opened arms, gave him the run of the Society's grounds, and set up a lab for him where he could practice his alchemy. Rapp was looking desperately for a sign, and he must have seen the Lion of Judah as his messenger from God. But the Lion was not good for the Harmonists and George Rapp. Not only did a large number of Society members follow Count de Leon down river, they demanded severance pay from the Society and eventually this settlement cost Rapp and the Society a quarter of a million dollars.

Unfortunately, the Lion of Judah wasn't as good at taking care of business as he was at fomenting discord, and soon he and a handful of followers left for Louisiana. This means, of course, that I could have almost been a Cajun, if I had actually had ancestors among the Economites. I was so close to so many possibilities infinitely more interesting than the truth and my family. The Lion's followers who did not go down the muddy Mississippi eventually settled throughout what's now known as Beaver Valley. Some probably still live in Monaca, which Phillipsburg became. Others lived in Beaver Falls, a town founded by Economy business interests (and best known for giving us Joe Namath) and still others became farmers in the hills above Economy. This is where my hope began. I wanted my

Schaeffer ancestor, my grandmother's great-great grandfather, to have succumbed to his carnal desire and followed the Lion of Judah to Phillipsburg. That's where my research began too.

The Rappites were record keepers. They knew who came to the Society and who left and when. When one joined the Society, he (or she) was supposed to give all his property and money to the group. The Society's ledgers recorded when a member left, the date of departure, the years in the Society, and what severance payment (if any) was given. Therefore, I found a Schaeffer, my Schaeffer I thought, named Jacob who left Economy March 6, 1832. He was paid $875 for his efforts in the Society. The Phillipsburgers turned out to be die hard record keepers too. I found out that Jacob Schaeffer married Katherine Staiger and that a baby was born April 18, 1833. Jacob was a dyer by trade. Just for good measure I also know that he lived in house number 25 and he shared this no doubt humble abode with two of his sisters, his mother-in-law, and his younger brother-in-law. Close quarters.

I knew this also. My great grandfather on my grandmother's side of the family was named John W. Shafer (Schaeffers come as Schafer, Shafer, Shaffer, and maybe some other spellings too) and he was born in November of 1861. His oldest brother, Jacob, was born in 1852. Everything was fitting together. I even found a Jacob Shafer in the Baden, PA, 1900 census. I couldn't find Baby Schaeffer's name, but if he too was named Jacob, a first-born son named after his father, then he would be the right age to father my Schaeffer line and connect me to Economy. How many Jacob Schaeffers (Shafers) could be running around Beaver County in 1833? Here's the problem. I'm a writer. This was sort of a mystery, a quest tale. If I were a scientist, even an historical researcher, I was violating a cardinal principle. I knew what I wanted to find. I was driven by desire. When I found facts that furthered my desire, I believed them whole heartedly. I was shoring fragments against my ruin.

But still it fit. I like to think that most of us would have believed we had found the ancestral link. I had nurtured this desire over a good deal of time and as the "facts" fell into place, my passion increased. I was sure I was on the right trail. I read histories of Economy, of the Harmonists. I joined the Beaver County Genealogical Society. I had them search census and property records. I had them send me graveyard records.

The Society, despite the schism, flourished into the 1890s. It owned a lot of property, extensive farmland, mines, oil wells, textile mills and other industrial properties. Economy was situated on the road heading north from Pittsburgh that followed the Ohio River. Soon, the railroad followed this road and the Society owned a substantial part of the railroad too. The Society ran an inn on its fortuitous site. It made, in short, a ton of money. But given that most of the Economy members did play by the rules, there were few little Economites. The Society had in its early years encouraged people to join the ranks and had adopted children into the group too, but in later years these policies ceased.

The Society was willing to officially give up sexual intercourse and procreation, but not amassing capital and wealth. This immense contradiction has attracted me too. If you can't take it with you, and in their case, you can't hand it down to your children either, why did they desire such wealth? Suffice to say, that Economy, or the Harmonists, were quite wealthy and owned much of Beaver County even as their membership grew smaller and smaller. Eventually, after a number of deaths and through a couple of back room deals, there were only two Harmonists left and they, John Duss and his wife, owned the whole, extensive, pie. They owned lots of pies. This is where the modern history of my hometown, my family, my personal mythology, even my poetry begins.

The Duss family sold most of the Harmonist's Economy property to the Berlin Iron Works, which became American Bridge, and American Bridge started a mill and a mill town named for itself—Ambridge. Next to Ambridge there's a little borough called Harmony, next to that my hometown of Baden and in the hills above all of this is the borough of Economy. Duss, as rich Americans are wont to do, took his money and ran off to Florida. American Bridge spawned the steel industry, became U.S. Steel and was joined by Jones and Laughlin and other steel fabrication plants and what I know of my life was born. My existence, I wanted to think, was brought about because I had ancestors who wanted sex more than their communal and religious ties and that this larger group that my ancestor had abandoned gave birth in a capitalist, maybe slightly criminal, maybe asexual way to a whole culture of steel mills, bridges, barges, soot and ash. I wanted to be an intimate, blood descendant, of all of this. I wanted to be able to see and touch a place and people that I had come from.

This desire to belong might have been fueled by the lack of belonging and connection my family has shown since the beginning of my family memory. No one knows (or will tell me) how my grandfather came from Ohio and met my grandmother. No one has told me why he quit whatever job he had to marry my grandmother and settle in her small town instead of wherever he was living. I don't know why my grandparents and I were Catholic and my aunts and their kids Protestants. I'm convinced that my grandfather's children did not like him. I'm pretty convinced that my father's siblings didn't like him either. But no one in my family talked about anything or anyone.

The End of Myth, The Intrusion of Truth

In a very tangible and yet mythological sense, I loved the Beaver Valley and Pittsburgh. I still do. Florida's a beautiful land, a little paradise really. But I wasn't born in Paradise, I was born in the Beaver Valley. Perhaps I should have seen the truth coming. There were holes in my research, but my desire for this extended family blinded me. I wanted this. It wasn't quite the passion of love, as in I can have this affair and not get in any trouble. There wasn't that price to pay. But I did want this, and my passion made possibility look like fact.

My whole house of cards was built on baby Schaefer, as he was known then. Born in 1833, about 13 months after his family left Economy, I needed his middle name to be Jacob and I needed him to, for some reason, decide he would call himself by his middle name once he was grown and about to father my great-great grandfather. In truth, I don't know what happened to baby Shaffer. He's listed on the Phillipsburg 1850 census, but not on the 1860 census. In 1860 he would have been 27 and could have left to start his own family, but where did he go. Apparently, what he did not do was start my family.

This is where another set of facts, a missile on or off course, entered this fiction and maybe changed it to non-fiction. When Oedipus sent for Laius' herdsman, he didn't want the terrible truth he was calling into his life. My Aunt Fran, being a good woman with a desire to be helpful, told Pat Shafer (my grandmother's niece) that I was trying to trace our Shafer family's roots.

If your only tool is a hammer, you see every problem as a nail. Cousin Pat was working from a more objective angle. She did not care a whit about the Harmony Society and its obsession for record keeping. In fact, when I told her over the phone, late one night, in a very strange conversation, what I knew of Shafers through the Harmony books, she didn't even know that Old Economy, as we know the Society, had a museum and archives. I was feeling somewhat smug when I told her how I'd found a baby Shafer born in 1833 that could have been our ancestor, but she wasn't buying it. She said no, our Jacob Shafer came to America from Wurtermberg, Germany, around 1840. This is where I gave in, surrendered. I knew that I did not have any research, only fragments sewn together by desire. I had a patchwork quilt, but I also knew that I had never learned to sew.

Pat sent me some documents that seemed to back her claims. At least she had the names right, no mysterious unnamed babies formed her cornerstone. According to Pat, our Jacob Shafer was born in 1823 and died in 1893 in Economy Borough (not the Harmony Society's Economy, but its namesake rural hills.) He was married to Catherine McAlay and their first child was born in perhaps 1852. This child too would be named Jacob. A number of other children followed, including my great grandfather John

William Shafer. The weight of Pat's evidence, compared to the flimsiness of mine, overwhelmed me. Looking back today, I don't know how she found out that our Jacob came here when he did, but she had so many good links in her chain of evidence, and I didn't have any chain at all.

I had to admit, reluctantly, that I was about to fail in my quest. I didn't have the strength to argue with Cousin Pat's findings, but I am struck by the great number of coincidences. First, and obviously, my real (according to Cousin Pat) patriarch was named Jacob just as my desired patriarch was. Both came from around Wurtermberg (but so did most of the German settlers around Economy.) The false Patriarch was married to Katharine and his sister was Katherine Shaffer. My Jacob married a Catharine and my grandmother was named Catharine.

Maybe I'm guilty of thinking all Smiths or Garcias are related. Shaffer (and its myriad spellings) is a very common German name. This is an unrequited love song. I gave Jacob Schaefer my heart and he stomped on it.

Creation Mythology

In Norris' poem, the man who thinks he's Welsh, the man who has desired so much to be from Wales, constructs a personal mythology that allows him, in his heart and mind, to be a Welshman. It's easy for Norris to see that this man is no more from Wales than were Columbus and Magellan. But Norris, a consummate gentleman, I've been told, decides why should I bother this guy with the truth? What good would it do? If he wants so much to be Welsh, then let it be so. It's not the same as any number of very white students who tried to find enough Indian ancestry somewhere to qualify for scholarships and other aid. "I should have known you anywhere ... for a Welshman," Norris generously told him, and the old man walked off into the night happy and content. Norris too, probably felt good.

Cousin Pat thinks she did well because she enlightened me, set me on the true path and let me know who my Shafer ancestor truly was. I didn't need that. I needed a cosmic Norris to sweep in and make that Schaefer in House 25 in Phillipsburg, my progenitor. Someone should have known me anywhere for a descendant of Economy. After all, I was there in 4th grade, 1962. That's more than half a lifetime, and unlike Norris' visitor, I have the right name. On paper this could have been true. Cousin Pat was all the messengers Oedipus summoned rolled into one. And I was Oedipus, though I swear I did not kill my father, or do anything nasty with my mother.

Creation myths tell us how the world came to be, how it was created and ordered. If Jacob Schaefer, lapsed Harmonist, did not play a part in my birth and isn't an ancestor, it's pretty much true that the Harmony Society and Economy created most of what I am, where I was born and raised. When John Duss and his wife succeeded in being the last Harmonists, and all that remained of the Harmonist holding became theirs, they sold the land around Economy's main buildings and grounds and it became American Bridge. American Bridge and U.S. Steel and Jones and Laughlin Steel and Armco created the steel mill economy and the life all of my neighbors, friends, and fathers knew. Railroads, mines, oil wells—the slick, dirty Ohio—that was all I knew when I was young and pretty much all I had to write about when I decided I wanted to be a writer.

What good would it have done if I had realized my quest? My life, that has seen a lot of contradiction and a good deal of backsliding, would have been brought about by a larger contradiction and a fundamentally greater backslide. I could have been descended from someone who said, you know what, that celibacy idea, it just doesn't work for me anymore.

When I was writing this essay, Old Economy hosted an exhibit called Out of Harmony for those who were descended from the Harmonist Society. Over a thousand people left the Society in its more than one hundred years of existence and this reception was calling the wayward flock home. I wanted very much to be in that number.

I'm not a total fool though; I was not going to try to pass for a Harmonist. I'd been burned once already in this quest. If I had gone to this celebration, I would have had to watch in passive resignation, and then stroll alone through Rapp's garden, thinking about how close I had come, as the twilight descended on Economy's ordered grounds.

Becoming Bedouin: Daughter, Teacher, Sister

Maryah Converse

"What's that ajnabiyya doing on the bus to Faiha'?"
"That's no foreigner! That's our daughter, Maryah al-Harahsheh."

i. The Village Faiha'

When Peace Corps Jordan placed me in a small hilltop village in the north, I went intending to teach English and learn Arabic in return. In my Peace Corps interview, I had requested to serve Arab families, a culture foreign and considered antagonistic to my own by some. It was April 2004, just after the invasion of Iraq to the east. The people of little Faiha' upended my assumptions, and I unsettled at least some of theirs. That I had expected.

I never expected to become one of them.

Before I arrived, the school headmistress made it known across the small, sprawling village that I was to be treated with the respect due her own daughters. The lines of family loyalty in Arab culture are both malleable and absolute. By her declaration, I was family, completely and indisputably, and the rules were clear to everyone in town. Disrespect me and you disrespected the headmistress and all the neighboring households.

Families were tight-knit in Faiha'. My little white cinder-block house was flanked by those of the headmistress, her sister Umm Anis, and their uncle, who was also their father-in-law—the sisters had married brothers from among their cousins.

Families were also large. Umm Anis and her husband Abu Anis were the parents of a son Anis, seven years old when I arrived; a daughter Alya, fifteen; a daughter Aaliya, thirteen; a son Hamza, five; a daughter Noor, three; and a baby on the way. And me.

The headmistress did treat me like a daughter, fed me whenever I dropped by, occasionally summoned me to help her with chores or cooking. Yet, though it took me longer to recognize the bond we were building, it was her sister Umm Anis who really made me feel like family.

ii. Umm Anis

She was my same average height, which in rural Jordan made us tall women. She was active, not skinny but slender. Like even the old grandmothers in the village, Umm Anis was limber from living all her life in households where the furniture was mostly *fershaat*—raw wool ticks or synthetic foam mattresses on the floor, with matching pillows against the walls behind and bolsters over the seams between. Women generally sat upright, their legs crossed in their skirts or stretched out straight under a light blanket, while men lounged on one hip against a bolster, knees and feet pulled up under their caftans. In the semi-nomadic Bedouin households of Umm Anis's great-grandmothers, those bolsters were camel saddles.

One Friday afternoon, less than a month after I moved to Faiha', Umm Anis had pulled the *fershaat* out onto the cool tile of the side porch, where she preferred to spend her time during spring and summer. It was south-facing and roofless with the prevailing easterly wind usually blowing across the porch end-to-end. The side porch was a perfect venue for relaxing and chatting over a pot of strong, sweet black tea, poured into little gold-rimmed glasses over sprigs of fresh sage or thyme from the garden at the tile's edge.

Abu Anis was home for the first lazy afternoon since I had moved in next door. He was a loud, friendly man who worked for the Ministry of Energy. He had been escorting a German telecom team for the last few weeks while I began to settle into the neighborhood. In part because of his perfect English, he was often away for weeks at a time, accompanying foreign consultants and contractors.

He was telling us about his trip and the incomprehensible things that foreigners do. He told me his stories mostly in English, though it was clear that Umm Anis could follow along. And he had a burning question from his trip. "These German guys said they don't believe in God. A lot of foreigners tell me they don't believe in God. Is that possible? Do you believe in God?"

"Well ..." I hesitated. I had often had this conversation as an agnostic kid in rural America, and I had my arsenal of answers prepared. But that schoolgirl had been snarky, defensive, combative, often angry, and her American classmates understood atheism, even if they found it morally repugnant.

It seemed incomprehensible to Abu Anis that anyone could lack a basic belief in God. I hedged, avoiding the choice between a conciliatory lie and too much truth. "I know many Americans and Germans who believe in God," I said.

He saw right through my carefully worded response. "That's not what I asked," said Abu Anis with a shake of his head. "I asked if you believe in God. Not other Americans. You."

I took a deep breath, thinking about the day in training when the Country Director said, "As an employee of the United States government, I can't ask you about your religion. So, I'm just going to recommend that, unless you're Muslim, tell people you're Christian when they ask. And they will ask!" Another day, after I had asked a staff member a question about the differing stories of Abraham in the Old Testament and the Qur'an, the director said, "I won't ask you if you're Jewish, but if you tell people in Jordan that you're Jewish, you'll be answering difficult questions about Israel all the time. It's probably better to say you're Christian."

Fresh out of training, though, I wasn't entirely ready to bend to this cultural norm yet. That defensive, self-righteous kid was not so far removed from my present self as I wanted to believe.

Looking Abu Anis in the eye, I shrugged, "Well, no. I don't believe in God."

They stared at me. I could see a dozen questions in Umm Anis's eyes that we didn't have enough shared language to discuss. Abu Anis said, "But how is that possible? Ya'ni—I mean, where do you think the world came from, if it wasn't created by God? Where did human beings come from?"

23

"*Ya'ni*, I guess I believe in science," I said, a little taken aback. I expected Abu Anis—well educated, with his perfect English and exposure to other cultures—to have a less literal interpretation of creation.

I spoke of geology and physics. I struggled to put my explanations into a combination of my broken Arabic and simple English that Abu Anis would understand. He looked more and more concerned for my soul, a look I knew well from my childhood in Bible country. I started to sense that I had made a mistake, had admitted to something I should have lied about, had maybe even torpedoed my chance for effective service to the families of Faiha' before it had begun.

Then I heard laughing voices approaching around the corner of the house. "This conversation is over," said Umm Anis softly. "The children are coming."

I don't know what Umm Anis said to her husband later. Although Abu Anis would occasionally explain elements of Islam to me over the next two years, he never again asked about my personal beliefs.

Perhaps, though, it was my unflinching honesty that brought out the same in Umm Anis.

One day, I was walking home from school with her oldest daughter, ninth grader Alya. It was about two miles back to our homes, and I relished the twice-daily exercise. Parents and teachers found my desire to walk strange, but the village children loved to accompany me along the way.

This particular midday, Faiha' was easing into the dry, blustery heat of summer, though its cinderblock construction still kept the school on the cool side. Halfway home, I began to regret the jacket I had worn out of the building.

"What are you doing?" asked Alya sharply.

My brow crinkled in surprise. "Taking off my jacket. It's hot."

Later that day, I dropped by Umm Anis's house. Alya had told her about our walk home. "You can't do that," Umm Anis said.

I was confused. "It was just my jacket, that's all."

"No. You can't do that. Don't do it again." She clicked her tongue with that upward jerk of the chin that in Jordan says more clearly than anything, "No, and no arguing."

I came to rely on Umm Anis to tell me what I needed to know, without holding back, kind but firm. She taught me to navigate her culture just as she taught her children, but with the respect of a sister who knew I didn't have to be told twice. I depended on her to correct a mistake once and never mention it again, knowing I had understood the gravity of her words.

iii. Privacy and Loneliness

Umm Anis did not wield the same obvious power and bold public opinions her sister displayed, but she was still a quiet power in her world—in her family, her household, her neighborhood. With sharp eyes and ears, and an army of nieces and nephews, Umm Anis missed nothing.

I was sitting on the *fershaat* on her side porch again with Umm and Abu Anis. The girls made us a pot of tea, poured over sprigs of mint fresh from the garden at our outstretched feet.

They were speaking sporadically in Arabic, in the casual manner of couples who have been together long enough to be comfortable with each other's silence. I wasn't really listening, letting my mind wander as the Arabic washed over me.

My attention snagged when Umm Anis told Abu Anis about something that I had been doing in my living room the day before. She never made eye contact or any indication I was sitting right there. I didn't let on that my Arabic was good enough to understand.

Abu Anis gave her a sharp look. "And how do you know what she was doing inside her house?" he asked.

"Well," she shrugged, "I watch her through her windows."

The Bedouin are traditionally a communal culture. Arabic doesn't have a word for "privacy." The women and girls I knew in Faiha', daughters of a desert heritage where being separated from your tribe meant death, were terrified of being alone. So was everyone they knew. From their perspective, it was clearly human nature, so obviously I must be afraid of solitude, too.

Especially in those first few months in Faiha', I heard this often. "Aren't you afraid? Don't you worry that something might happen to you?"

Consequently, I was rarely alone. Sometimes it was middle sister Aaliya and her next-door cousin Aiat with their English homework, or younger kids asking endless questions about my family photos. Sometimes, it was their second cousins down the road, demanding that I do their homework for them, or give them something of mine that they desperately wanted. An older A-level student might chase out the younger ones so I could check their work on a practice test for the *tawjihi* school-leaving exam. Whenever I was home, there were children in my home.

After the sunset *adhaan* had rung out from the mosques, they would beg me to sleep at their houses. Especially at night, they worried that if they left me to sleep alone in my little house, I would be snatched by kidnappers. Or attacked by feral dogs. Or poisoned by the little pink gecko that lived at the top of my bedroom walls. They had a dozen reasons why I should be afraid.

After a while, I discovered that the constant invasion of my space was encouraged by Umm Anis. She would look out of her window and into mine, then snag her daughter or niece and say, *"Yaa Haraam!*—Oh, woe! Poor Maryah! She's all alone in her house. She must be terrified! You'd better go over there and keep her company."

"Just try to imagine," I said one day to her older daughter Alya, "living all day, every day in English. Speaking it, hearing it, trying to understand, to learn it. Imagine you're in America and no one speaks Arabic and you need English to eat, take the bus, at school, at home. All the time. Try to imagine it."

I watched Alya try to picture a life of English. I wonder if she, too, was thinking about my site visit, a month before I had moved into the house beside hers. On that first visit, she had been glued to my side as my interpreter and guide to Faiha', using every scrap and shard of English she had ever collected.

"Can you imagine it? Can you imagine how very tired that would make you, all English all the time?" I asked, even as I knew from experience that it was unimaginable.

She didn't reply, but her eyes spoke volumes.

"That's how I feel. I love you all, and I love your

company, and I love Arabic and want to learn it and live in it. But at the end of the day, I need two hours to myself, without people, without Arabic, just me."

To my surprise, it worked. I won some much needed evening introvert time, and it felt good to carve out that time for myself. Immersion in Bedouin culture made me really understand what solitude meant to me.

I could sit at the open window, listening to the kids play on the shared lawn, re-watching episodes of *Dark Angel*, or half of *Dances with Wolves*. I identified powerfully with the mutant girl hoping for love and acceptance in a post-apocalyptic barter economy, and the lonely colonizer in an uneasy truce with both his neighbors and his shifting moral universe.

After a couple weeks, I noticed that Umm Anis and her sister weren't summoning me to their uncle's house in the evenings anymore.

At first, I was relieved. Sometimes as many as ten adults squeezed into the ten-by-twelve-foot cinderblock box of a house. One had a fussy baby, another a grumpy sleep-drunk toddler, and eighteen other cousins ran in and out. They talked over the television, over each other, laughed loud and long. A cacophony of Arabic. Even when I wasn't listening, my brain was working overtime to process all the language around me.

Late one afternoon, Alya, Aaliya and their next-door cousin Aiat were finishing up some homework when Aaliya asked, "Why don't you come to Grandpa's after sunset anymore?"

Trying to deny my bruised feelings, I shrugged.

"Because you don't invite me anymore. You used to shout to me from the yard every night."

They gave me an affectionately confused look I would come to know well. Alya, a little older and my self-appointed cultural translator, shook her head. "You don't need an invitation."

My childhood of introverted New England reserve had not prepared me for this. "My mother always says, you never drop in on someone without an invitation."

"Just come over," Alya said, still shaking her head at my silly foreign ways. "You're family."

Sometimes I did. And sometimes Alya or her sisters or brothers would knock or shout from the yard to invite me, just to be sure I was included.

iii. Afternoon Routines

Once my evenings were sorted, it was not long before afternoons became a new, different sort of tension.

I was encouraged to design an after-school English program, and I tried a few failed experiments with an empty room of my little house in those first few months. An English conversation class, a grammar enrichment class for the university-bound, an afterschool homework clinic.

Eventually, everyone's enthusiasm for such initiatives petered out until I was down to just two dedicated disciples and a familiar routine. After lunch, Aaliya and her next-door cousin Aiat would show up with their English homework. Despite their best attempts at persuading me to just give them answers, eventually they realized I was always going to make them work for their educations. Once convinced, though, they worked diligently and made noticeable progress in both what they learned, and how.

Sometimes, though, they showed up before I had finished eating, or before I had even finished cooking. Or they showed up later than usual, after I had decided to clean my bathroom with the unexpectedly free afternoon. I would say, "I can't help you right now, I'm sorry. Can you come back in an hour?" They would give me that familiar bemused look, then walk away.

Suddenly, Umm Anis and her next-door sister-in-law were knocking on my door. "Did you tell our daughters that you can't help them with their homework today?"

"No," I said slowly. "I just asked them to come back later. I'm in the middle of scrubbing my toilet."

"Now, Maryah," said Umm Anis, gently but firmly, "if you really want to live as an Arab among the Arabs, like you say you do, there's something you need to understand about the Arabs. When someone asks you for help, you don't ask them to come back when it's more convenient for you. You stop what you're doing and help, right away. That's what we do."

"Okay." I paused, collected my thoughts. This made sense for the lone traveler seeking assistance in the Arabian desert. "But when someone asks you for help, and you're in the middle of cleaning, you have one or three daughters who will finish cleaning while you help. When your daughters ask me for help and I'm in the middle of cooking dinner, if I stop, my dinner burns. I don't have anyone else to finish the job, and then I don't eat."

They looked at each other and me, pondering. They didn't know a single person other than me who lived alone and had never really paused to consider the practical implications. "We'll let you finish," they finally said.

Umm Anis began sending one of her kids across the rocky ground between our homes at least three times a week with a plate of whatever she was serving to her family for the large midday meal. She sent Anis with a plate for his grandparents' lunch almost every day, too, so it took me months to connect my meals back to our conversation.

I was faster to hear about another effect of this conversation. "Poor Maryah, *yaa Haraam*" she began saying to her nieces and nephews and the other neighborhood children. "She lives alone with no one to help with cooking and housework. When she does something nice for you, like helping you with your English homework, you should be doing something to help her, too."

Now, when Aaliya and Aiat came with their homework and I was still eating, they pushed me out of the kitchen to finish my lunch while they washed all my dishes and made tea. Only then would we sit down to do their English homework together.

One day, Aaliya asked, "Do you think it would be okay if we brought our math and science homework, too?"

"I don't know if I can help you with that," I hedged.

"Oh, we know that. It's just so quiet here. It's nice."

My teacher heart grew two sizes that day.

iv. Ramadan

Umm Anis's last month of pregnancy was the Muslim holy month of fasting from food and water from first light to sunset. It didn't slow her down. Quite the opposite. Her sister worked almost as many hours as ever at school, without food or drink, supervising teachers who also weren't eating, and kids who were mostly fasting, too. Umm Anis seemed compelled to compensate for her sister's long afternoon naps. After her own early nap, Umm Anis would be in the kitchen, creating massive quantities of rice-heavy main dishes, as well as salads and sides, fresh rosewater and lemonade, and special Ramadan desserts drenched in simple syrup.

Ramadan is also a time for visiting with family, and on at least half the twenty-eight nights of the fast, there were aunts, cousins, grandparents and more distant family visiting from out of town. Her in-laws often hosted the guests after dinner, but Umm Anis provided most of the food. Her daughters, sister and sisters-in-law helped, but Umm Anis was quietly in charge. In Ramadan, the housewives in Faiha' also sent their kids around to all their neighbors with plates of whatever they were cooking, but Umm Anis's plates were a little fuller, a little more sumptuous. She was an excellent cook.

Near the end of Ramadan, Umm Anis had her baby, a girl they eventually named Siddeen. Nursing mothers are exempt from the fast, but everyone else was fasting. Even her youngest children, though not required, insisted on trying to fast three-quarter days "like a grownup!"

On her first afternoon back in Faiha', Umm Anis sent her youngest to fetch me to the family room. "I know you're fasting to understand us better," she said, "and that's a good thing. But you're not fasting for God and your faith. Will you break your fast with me? It's lonely to eat by myself."

And so, I didn't quite fast for all of Ramadan.

v. Winter

The dry desert heat gave way to daily downpours and temperatures dipping towards freezing. My single propane space heater barely took the edge off the cold in my uninsulated cinderblock house. I wore layer upon layer of thick cotton and wool, slept in my clothes, and spent most of my days under a duvet thick with raw wool. Some afternoons, though, I would be invited to Umm Anis's family room for supper and a telenovela with the family.

Umm Anis had two large space heaters and seven or more bodies spending most of the day and night on plush carpet and thick *fershaat* in her family room. I became more comfortable with inviting myself over, reveling in the opportunity to leave a sweater or two hanging by her side door on my way in. One of the daughters would slip into the kitchen to make the ubiquitous pot of sweet black tea. Umm Anis might be helping her sons with their English homework.

I rarely heard her speak English, and never more than a couple words at a time, but Umm Anis knew the elementary textbooks inside and out. When my aunt, a monolingual American, came to visit me in Faiha', she and Umm Anis were fast friends before I even had the chance to introduce them. Each speaking her own language. Somehow they understood each other perfectly.

For the village of Faiha' and I, understanding each other was an unending frustration and delight. "Why do you always wear socks?" asked Aaliya one afternoon. Everyone looked up. They all regularly dashed back and forth across the shared lawn in plastic shower shoes, even in an early morning dusting of snow, and often a mismatched pair not their size that slipped off frequently on the uneven ground.

My thick wool L.L. Bean boot socks, by contrast, never left my feet, even in sleep. "My mother always says, when your feet are warm, the rest of you is warm."

"Are you listening?" Umm Anis pointed out quickly to her five lounging children. "When you ask Maryah a question, what does she say? How often does she start with, 'My mother always says...'? Why can't you be more like Maryah and listen to your mother?"

Like any well-loved child might, they rolled their eyes and pretended to ignore their mother.

"Have you prayed yet?" Umm Anis might ask her children while I visited. "Get up and pray."

One of the girls would get up, pull on a long seersucker skirt with a one-size-fits-all elastic waistband over her pajama pants, and drape her whole upper body in a matching seersucker *khimaar* prayer shawl. She pulled a prayer rug down off the top of the television and lay it on the carpet facing an empty section of the long eastern wall of the family room.

I was deeply touched by this ritual every time I witnessed it. Prayer in Islam is meant to be done in community. In this particular setting, though, it always felt intimate, an indication of their ease at my intrusion into their daily lives and practices.

Then the next daughter would go, and then the little one side-by-side with her littler brother.

Another rainy winter evening, I left my dripping wool cape and coat by the door, but kept my long wool knit jacket over a short wool sweater. Umm Anis had a new diesel stove heating the family room, and I was quickly too hot. I peeled off the jacket. The sweater underneath was a slim fit and ended just above the hip, but with only Umm Anis and her children around, it was modest enough.

I knew that Abu Anis had been away for nearly two weeks, escorting another team of foreign engineers around Jordan. "When will he be back?" I asked.

"Tonight, *inshallah*," said Umm Anis. God willing. I knew she had been missing him.

Later, when I heard the front door open, I grabbed my long knit jacket, pulling it back on. It was their next-door cousin Aiat, borrowing a cup of sugar. I slipped out of my jacket again.

Umm Anis peered sharply at her daughters. "Did you see that? Maryah heard the door and thought your father was coming home, and she put her jacket back on. Why can't you be more like Maryah? She's a better Muslim than you are!"

Her niece and daughters rolled their eyes and smiled.

vi. Spring

The following spring, Aaliya asked me one day over her English homework, "Do you think we could have lunch here with you?" When I hesitated, Aiat jumped in to add, "We'll bring all the ingredients! We'll just cook it here, in your kitchen, and then we can do homework."

We started cooking together every couple of weeks. I taught them how to make Kraft macaroni and cheese and introduced them to peanut butter and Nutella. They taught me how to make *baba ghanoush* and *galayat bandourah*—stewed tomatoes. Aaliya and Aiat spread out newspapers on the floor, put out the food and big flat rounds of bread, and we ate together. Then they would wash dishes and all the floors in the house before we sat down to do English homework.

Once, they got my permission to have a bigger party, inviting all their girl cousins to my house, including the headmistress's eldest daughter Ala'. They kept begging me to make more food. "One more box of macaroni!" and "Just open one more can of clotted cream!" and I kept saying, "No. It will be enough." I couldn't predict when or how often Umm Anis would feed me, so I tried not to have leftovers in my fridge. My mother hates to waste food, and too many families right there in Faiha' had too little.

Finally, we all sat down to eat. Everyone ate their fill, with not a scrap of food left before us. The girls started whispering to each other, watching me with side-eyes, tittering.

"What? What's going on?"

"You're more *sunna* than us!" giggled Aaliya.

Sunna, I knew, is the example of the Prophet Mohammad and the first Muslim community in Medina, how they dressed and cut their hair and treated each other. It is the template for how all Muslims should behave. But I didn't understand the connection. "What do you mean?"

They tittered, and finally Ala' gathered her first-year university student dignity and explained, "The Prophet Muhammad, peace be upon him, said you should never cook more food than you can eat in one sitting. They didn't have refrigerators fourteen hundred years ago, you know, so it wasn't safe. But our mothers always make twice as much as we need and keep plates of leftovers in the fridge. You always make exactly as much food as you're going to eat, just like today. You're more *sunna*—a better Muslim than we are."

vii. Bedouin

Most Saturday afternoons, after picking up macaroni and Nutella at the big Safeway in the nearest city, I would be sitting towards the back of the mid-sized bus, waiting for it to be full enough to depart. Sometimes, a local man would stick his head in, take a long look at me, and ask the bus driver, "What's that *ajnabiyya* doing on your bus? What could she possibly want in Faiha'?"

"Ajnabiyya?" All three of the drivers always clicked their tongues in the same dismissive fashion, always had the same easy response. "That's no foreigner! She's our daughter, Maryah al-Harahsheh."

After Peace Corps, my mother said, "When we visited you in Faiha', we could see you had a family and good friends there. But Umm Anis was your mother and your sister, the one who really took care of you."

Without her, I would not be Maryah al-Harahsheh.

Being Home

Susan Delgado Watts

Every day when all the morning housekeeping chores are complete, I travel to the small room that I refer to as my office and my bead room. The sun rises from the east side of the house in the early morning hours. The room slowly lights up allowing me to turn off the lamps. I take advantage of the light of this little room and will try to make a piece of jewelry. The walls contain me and my many bead trays. The colorful beads beckon me to take them from their trays and create something beautiful. My hot coffee sits on the table with a fresh dollop of whipped cream. The aroma from the coffee tickles my nose tempting me to just sit and drink the hot liquid. But my mind nudges me to be productive. The beads are large, small, oval, rectangular, circular. Each with its own unique coloring. They sit amongst themselves waiting, pleading quietly, for my fingers to pick them up and release them from their small square confined spaces.

The beads like being threaded, wired, attached, strung, connected with headpins and clasps, and fashioned in a way that will allow them to hang from someone's ear lobes, neck, or wrists. The wearing of a piece of jewelry allows others to admire the beads and for the beads to have purpose. Sometimes, I am successful at creating. Sometimes, my imagination is lost, and I fail. And when I fail, I take the beads apart and put them back into their small assigned spaces. The beads then have to wait silently like sentinels for me to pick them up again.

My small bead room and office also houses my collection of poetry books, novels, cookbooks, writing books, gem books, crafting paper, ribbons, mini drill, jewelry tools. The morning sunlight is soothing for my soul. I listen to classical music. Think. Daydream. Make notes on 4 x 6 cards of what I might write. Or notes to remind me of a birthday or anniversary, or to reach out and talk to someone. It is a room where small things are created and ideas float in the air, waiting for me to look up and capture one, like when you smell a flower and its essence is registered in your brain. You implant a memory of it and hope to remember it another time.

In the later part of the morning, the sun will change positions. When this happens, the room gets shadowed and dark, like a cave, so I get up from my table and travel the short distance to the living room. This is where the sun now shines from the west over our tiled roof. The living room is inviting and it's as though I have traveled miles to see the sun again.

The living room walls light up brightly in all the whiteness. I open the windows hoping that a breeze will travel between them. The mourning doves coo in the ratty half dead tree in the corner of the front yard. It should really be taken out of the ground, but the doves have found this tree acceptable for their nests. I look out the open window and hear their melodies among the half-dead tree limbs and fallen leaves. Because of them, I do not remove the tree from the yard. It doesn't compare well to the neighbors' trimmed green trees looking hardy. Our tree is scrawny, but it has a purpose: doves.

The white sofas, red chair, dark end tables, and ottoman brighten with the sun's arrival into the living room. Every piece of furniture becomes softer, more comfortable, more inviting for someone to sit on. The room whispers, enticing a person to contemplate, observe, read, or write, illuminated by the sunlight. I can sit and look out the large window, see the trees, fallen leaves, tall green grasses, and weeds across the street. Time spent in the living room carries a different meaning from that spent in my office-bead room.

As the large white Casablanca fan rotates slowly with its wide blades, I become reflective. She is a house that we happened upon by accident. We had moved several times within a year as our beach house sold very quickly once it hit the market. This house seduced us with her mountain vistas and her good bone structure. There she stood empty of all furniture waiting silently as my husband and I dialed the number on her For Sale sign. We made an appointment to walk inside her walls and explore her empty belly. That same afternoon we made an offer, and thirty days later, the real estate agent gave us the keys to her front door. She welcomed us with silence. She needed minor work, repairs, paint, and new carpet to make her livable. She became our home and we filled her insides with just enough furniture.

I have kept my emotions in check because I do not want to get attached to her. We arrived at a time of great personal loss and not knowing the future of our life journey.

Her walls are not adorned with pictures of family or art. There is no color. She is adorned simply with a couple of small pictures of our daughters, and one piece of artwork.

I sit in the living room's glow and memories flood past. My mind travels to places that I have been over the years when there were no restrictions on travel or being with people, drinking in bars or eating quiet meals in restaurants. Before, we could get on a plane and travel to explore new countries, new lands. But now we are all limited in where we can go. The living room becomes my container for a few hours.

My eyes take in the scene across the street and I search for words that I might turn into a story or an essay. What am I curious about at the moment? Where should I travel in my fantasies? What has really happened in my days that I am willing to write about? In my dreams? My insecurities? My dark thoughts?

The breeze coming through the window moves a few loose stray strands of my black hair tickling my nose to remind me that I am actually sitting in a white chair with my feet up on a white ottoman and not on an airplane heading to a new destination. Time, confinement, limitations, space, have become intimate friends and enemies all at once. There are days now that I can only muster the energy to write one sentence on a sheet of notebook paper, but my fountain pen has made doodles all over. Blue ink is a lovely color for doodles.

Some days, being at home allows the luxury of reading, doing the laundry, drinking coffee, and staying in my sleeping shirt all day long, my hair pulled up in a messy ponytail, no makeup on my face, not seeing friends or anyone in the world. The day is deliciously unproductive, but the feeling only lasts for a short time. Then the loss of connection in real time with real humans tugs at my brain and my heart, and I feel a sense of loss. Not being in the world with others, no writing classes, no outdoor symphony, no movies, no friends for lunch, no visits with sick friends, or early evening cocktails followed by dinner. The relaxation of talking, laughing, crying, connecting in person becomes a void. Time becomes my enemy. It cannot tick away fast enough for me to escape the yearning and longing for that missing part of life that I used to enjoy. Zoom on a computer, Facetime, these are not the same as touching and hugging a real person in real time. They cannot replace true human connection. Touch is lost for now.

There is rumbling on the street of black treaded tires, a noisy engine, and a square brown UPS truck stops in our driveway. It jars me back to the present. Again, I have not traveled from the white chair in the living room. The UPS man rings the doorbell. A package has arrived. The UPS man does not wait for me to open the red front door. He hops back into his brown truck and drives on to his next stop, robbing me of an opportunity to say hello to someone in the outside world. Time, for him, is precious. He has to make his quota of deliveries for the day. He doesn't have time for chit chat. I see the truck disappear as I get up from the white chair to retrieve the package. I wonder what has been ordered and if it will take me by surprise. These days, allowing the house to contain me has made me forgetful. I can't remember the day of the week or how much time has passed. It is a slight defect I have acquired from becoming a home body who only takes walks in the neighborhood or around the lake.

The package feels light, and my curiosity fades about

what its contents might be. I drop it on the hall table in the foyer to be opened later. I return to the chair in the living room. There is only so much time left in this day before the sun begins to move to the east and the living room becomes less inviting for reading, writing, or listening to music. I want to sit as long as possible before dusk arrives and forces me to turn on the lamps. The walls in the living room comfort me—another type of container for my being and my thoughts.

Six o'clock will arrive soon, and I will have to think about food. The day is getting cooler. The light is fading. I will have to get up and turn on lamps for light. What will I make for dinner? What can I prepare in fifteen minutes? What wine will complement the meal? These questions enter my thought process as I finish writing.

The sun's departure forces me into the kitchen, where the room becomes smaller and where I have become efficient in preparing meals. I am still able to look outside and see the mountains and watch the hundreds of black crows fly east to nest in the trees for the night.

I fantasize that someday I will have a big kitchen with plenty of cupboards, a large refrigerator, a walk-in pantry, and eight burners on the stove. Someday. But for now, I camp out in this little kitchen that has cupboards filled with glassware, dinner platters, food processor, food scales, plastic-ware, pots, bowls, silverware, napkins, everything I need to put dinner together for our family. For a kitchen this size, I double up on the storage and then quickly forget where I put things. It is a hazard with small spaces. Ironic, I know.

At dinner, we all gather and talk about our days. About the future and what each of us has on our minds. It's a time to unwind from being in our sheltered worlds working remotely from home. The small kitchen table makes intimacy's arrival comfortable for all of us.

The table is set with the fine silver, china, and wine glasses. I never want to be like my mother who saved all of the fine things, the good towels, chocolates, and wine for guests and our extended family when they came to visit. Being home now more than ever means that we must enjoy all the fine things we have acquired through the years. Drink the good wines and eat the best chocolates. Life needs to be enjoyed at all times, not just when company comes to visit.

Tonight, like every night, we will laugh, tell stories, talk about things that bother us, reflect about past times, eat, drink the wine slowly, and plan for the future. We will look out the big kitchen windows. I will get up and yell "goodnight crows," as they head east. And my family members will reply while sitting in the kitchen nook, "Goodnight crazy lady," and they will laugh at me. We will see the sky turn orange, blue, black with evening's arrival. And when everyone has filled their bellies and downed enough wine, the dishes will be cleared, the dishwasher loaded, and everyone will travel to the living room for a movie. Our talking will only be intermittent about whatever program is running and everyone will relax. Darkness will get darker, and the moon will get brighter, lighting the earth and the roads for those who must travel for jobs at night.

This little house welcomes anyone who needs a place to land. The red double doors in front open wide for anyone who needs to enter. Throughout our forty years of marriage my husband and I have had many teenagers, young adults, and mature adults stay with us, some going to school, some fresh out of college, some going through divorces. Every person was welcome. When I was growing up with abuse and alcohol in the home, there was not a welcoming house for me to go to. So, when I left home it was only natural for me to always have my doors open for anyone who needed four walls, comfort, a bed, and safe place to land.

When our daughters were in high school, we hosted Sunday night burritos. Any of their friends could sit down at six o'clock for dinner at our table. Back then, we had a large oval table made in Indonesia we picked up on our travels. It could seat twenty to twenty-four people with all the leaves inserted. The dinner etiquette rules were that everyone should come to the table with clean hands, no baseball caps on their heads, no cell phones, and each person had to be mentally present. Each had to put a cloth napkin across his or her lap and not on the table. They should use the silverware correctly, and contribute to the conversation with everyone else. After a couple of weeks of hosting these simple dinners, news spread that Sunday burrito night was great, and teenagers came faithfully to our house to share the meal. Some of them never had meals with their parents because both parents worked or just never set a time to have a meal with family members. This became our Sunday ritual throughout the high school years, through their summer breaks, Christmas breaks and when they would come home from college each year until all of them graduated. My husband and I watched all those young people grow into adults. Now they are all in the world, working real jobs.

Whenever a group of them are in town we still host burrito night. The wooden table we had for years was used so much it wore thin, and its oval top grew wobbly. In its place, we now have my husband's grandmother's table made of walnut that dates back to 1870. With its leaves inserted to expand it, the table has seen many years here on earth with many people enjoying meals, drinking wine, and telling stories. We bought new chairs to accommodate this particular style of table. Our old dining chairs needed constant repairs after rambunctious gatherings of friends.

Sometimes we host eight for burritos and sometimes we host twenty. It has become a tradition no matter the time of year. Now, even some of the parents attend burrito nights with their grown children. They, too, want to share a meal filled with banter, belly laughs, and stories as everyone vies for attention to tell their jokes. On top of all that, there is always the challenge to see who can eat the most burritos in one sitting. When people come together to share a meal and relax, in a place where they feel comfortable and safe there is room for all kinds of discoveries and time to share our hearts.

Though the dining room lacks any kind of flooring apart from a red rug underneath the table and chairs, it has not kept me from entertaining friends or young adults. I get teased by everyone asking "when are you going to put in the hardwood floors?" My reply is simple, "I like cement floors, because if anything gets spilled during dinner, they are easy to clean." The words are always spoken jokingly. Our grown daughters and their husbands would like to say one day that their mom finally got around to installing the hardwood floors. But for now, the cement will suffice. I use the silver, the china, and the fine linens, cook great meals, serve decent wine and use grandma's walnut table every chance I get.

At present, our house yearns for large gatherings. There are no dinner parties or burrito nights. There is no boisterous laughter ringing from the walls. I travel from one room to another observing our simple house. Each small bedroom has a watercolor painting hanging above the bed. Each one depicts somewhere we have traveled in the world. All were done by a local artist from La Jolla, California. The beds are adorned with simple white bed coverings and pillowcases, and even though there are four of us living together, the house lacks the music daily noise. It's lonely, just as I am on some days.

We still sit at grandma's table, but our stories and laughter can't fill the dining room all the way. The house will remain empty of laughter, clinking wine glasses, platters of hot food, and crashing water glasses being tipped over until such time as it is safe to travel outside our homes once again to gather with other people. Our house with its white walls, furniture, bead table, living room, bedrooms, dining room, and kitchen, keep us contained. She will continue to allow us to travel from room to room and invite our imaginations and fantasies to fill the days. She will continue to keep us safe. And time will continue to be our friend as well as our enemy. Meanwhile, I will continue to write words with my fountain pen on loose-leaf notebook paper. I will continue to keep a safe distance from her. I will acknowledge that she has been a good container for sheltering. She is a house and I am grateful to sit and write within her structure. And I have enjoyed and disliked being contained within her walls. I continue marking time, slowly, painfully, angrily, happily, and with resolve until I can go out again. In the meantime, I contemplate my next journey into another room.

Living Between the Leaves

John Flynn

My wife Angelica and I met in front of a library. We've
been married for 25 years and, if asked, we'd both say that
we are most at home inside of books. Mr. John Waldsmith
is another individual about whom I would say the same,
though I never asked him outright. We met at a flea market
just outside of Akron, Ohio, where he was selling stereoscope cards, stamps, old books and other forms of ephem-
era and memorabilia. In the end, we bought some books
from him for $3 a bag. I repaired two of them, a hobby of
mine, as a way to practice my skills with acid free paper
and adhesives. One book that I put into the bag was a
vintage edition of a novel by Washington Irving, a work I'd
never heard of before, let alone read. Mr. Waldsmith told
us how much he loved Irving and was saddened nobody
read him any longer.

Then he told us about his book, *Stereoviews: An Illus-
trated History and Price Guide*, which he'd written and published with Wallace-Homestead on the subject of stereoscope cards. He told us it was still in print and that it would
soon be released in a second edition, updated especially

for the Internet market with all the pricing changes that entails. He spoke as an expert. We were outdoors in the parking lot of what had been a beef and poultry auction complex, with agricultural exchange warehouse buildings, plenty of room for people to mill about, and the dealers at their own tables and chairs peddling second-hand goods. Waldsmith didn't look well; he was coughing constantly while he spoke to us, blowing his nose, sneezing, but I didn't think he was suffering a head cold, but rather that he was gravely ill and had grown accustomed to it.

He kept his distance, but he looked so pleased and surprised we'd chosen to spend time with him. He kept egging us on to pay cash for more items, though all we could afford, and wanted, were books. I would have bought stamps, which I also collect as a hobby, but they don't make me feel at home the way old tomes do, and his prices were beyond what I could meet at that time.

What we both liked about this man was that he didn't appear upset with our restraint. Nor did he run us off. His price for the bag of books had not been our idea, but his. We'd expected to pay a dollar for each book, but he kept encouraging us to take more and then said, "You can have the whole bag for three dollars." How can one not like such a bargain? Talk about cheap airfare back to the place where you were first born, and isn't this the sort of surprise a vagabond like myself wanders through flea markets in order to find?

It was an overcast day and we stood under a long narrow roof that extended off one of the ag buildings, part of what had once been a major trading and selling area. I found it easy to imagine cattle and sheep led along under that roof toward the large bay doors that allowed entry into a warehouse. I imagined farmers selling eggs and chickens they'd grown in those northern reaches of the Buckeye State. Now, like so much in America, it had become a sweeping yet empty enterprise, occupied a couple days a week in spring and summer (and maybe in winter, I didn't know) by mercenary gypsies, basically good people desperate to sell anything in any condition to pocket a few greenbacks. This kind of peddling had no doubt been profitable at one time, but with the onset of eBay and the education of consumers and sellers alike who follow such programs as Antiques Roadshow, any real bargains or innocent sales of stuff for the sake of getting rid of stuff had pretty much become a reflection of a bygone era.

Such sellers are shrewd. They sell on eBay themselves. They know what the Internet market will bring, so there's no way buyers like my wife and me are going to score the very deals the sellers scored when they'd bought their own goods to sell. I'd been going to flea markets since I was a boy and I'd seen the culture of such swapping and trading devolve into what I thought had become rather a crude vulture-upon-vulture interaction. This was what surprised me most pleasantly about meeting John Waldsmith. He didn't sneer at us and chase us off when we suggested we couldn't pay his price for something. Other dealers had done so in the many similar venues I'd visited over the years.

Mr. Waldsmith struck us both as remarkably intelligent, hardly one living out of his loaded van and driving off to the next flea in the next state and planning a return to Ohio on the following weekend. Knowing we weren't from those parts, and happy to see old books go to a caring home, he commented that no one read books anymore, no one bought them either, or even valued them. I'd had this same thought many times myself, and to hear someone else sound just as dismayed and slightly curmudgeonly about it, as I had, warmed my cockles a bit.

But I couldn't be homeless. I needed books. The homelier, the better. With their cracked spines and foxed pages and dusty aromas, they were easy to adopt and to value.

However, Waldsmith's negativity, his simmering anger over this, seen in his face, in the hardened tone of his voice, was startling. Neither coarse nor cruel, though anyone would deem him bitter upon hearing him speak, his voice was soft and his physical stature was that of a sparrow. He wasn't imposing at all, nor loud, but he was, without question, angry. His anger both scared and attracted me.

I didn't want to leave him. He wouldn't let us. He kept engaging my wife in conversation until she asked him if he had any novels by women authors from the early 20th Century who'd peaked in the 1920s. She had a list of these favorites, what she apologized for as a "guilty pleasure," labeling their work "chick lit that had become outdated." Whether it was the Southern romantic Temple Bailey, England's own Berta Ruck, or Frank Norris's sister-in-law, Kathleen Thompson Norris, my wife, whose first language was Russian, found the cultural references and the language in these rarities endearing and a comfort. They helped her feel at home. Perhaps Mr. Waldsmith had more stashed away somewhere. Certain volumes were quite difficult to find. She knew which ones had not been converted to E-books on the Gutenberg web page.

No, he said. He looked apologetic. These titles were all he had, and they were in such poor condition. To ask even a dollar each for them was a little too much. It wasn't like they could be read without falling apart. True enough, but what I revered were the thick gold gilt-edged pages, the leather covers, the embroidered gold lettering, the stamped lettering, the images inside the books. These were all tomes I could feel at home in, and even repair, and they would give another home-seeking bibliophile out there much pleasure.

Of course, they'd never be worth any big money, but must everything be about dollar value? This wasn't. Our tryst was about home and search and rescue and rehabilitation. None of these books had to go into an incinerator. I'd seen enough trashing of books as a volunteer at our local library's annual book sale, and I'd first learned book repair as a way to stem this somewhat. Books by the ton, if only people knew, get shipped off to the incinerator every month from nearly every local library in the country, in spite of well-intentioned efforts to salvage some profit through a Friends of the Library sale.

Do we only want to read screens all the time? I don't think so. The book, as artifact, has its own many lives and personalities, charms and enticements. Much depends on what its reader brings to it. As an obsessive reader and traveler in his sixth decade, books have grounded me as a form of home throughout my life. Why are we abandoning them, rushing headlong into all things digital? I don't know. I mourn this as yet another loss, with a corrosive effect on our shared humanity. In the poorer countries where I've lived, books and authors are lionized. Homeless doesn't only mean living on the street. It means an emptiness within, soullessness, an existential sob that wells up in the breast and cannot be mitigated.

We kept nosing through the man's dirty stacks, the

soggy cardboard boxes under his table, and we listened as Waldsmith loosened up and talked in the way that lonely people talk, getting it all out, unsure he'd have another chance to vent. We were eager listeners, attentive, and as someone who over the years has been paid to help book-sellers earn lots of money, I made short work of Wald-smith's inventory, knowing Book Club editions when I saw them, seeking only dry antiquated editions, or newer cop-ies that were clean and had dust jackets. I didn't find much of anything. I'd chosen to buy the man's discards, most of them damaged.

What wasn't damaged led me back to a question I'd often asked myself when working in bookstores, especially larger ones which sold both new and second-hand edi-tions. The question was: Why was this published, at all? How many millions of tons of paper each year goes into publishing absolutely dreadful forms of what, for lack of a better word, I'll call literature. I use that word solely in the meaning that the material is driven by written language, not visual. Novels, biographies, the like. I need not ex-plain. It leaves a sour burning in the bottom of my stomach when I see volume after volume of the same best-selling authors. Let me start with the Bible or the Koran, do we need more copies of those two tomes? Has anyone ever dared to say how much mass genocide, war and brutality those allegedly spiritual guidebooks have generated? *Mein Kampf* anyone? I know this will irk many, as it's meant to. As I'm writing from Turkey, if I dared express this in any public forum, I'd be guaranteeing my own expulsion from the country, if not my own death. Yes, believe it.

I don't think the quality of literature is dying out. It's more an end to an era once promulgated by the likes of

Harold Bloom, when to be a discerning and knowledgeable critic or reader was a noble calling. Nowadays, such pursuits are derided as a waste of time. The very elasticity and shape of minds is changing, a subject Nicholas Carr writes about in *The Shallows*, with the experience of absorbing long vertical text demanding too much rigor for those weaned on and accustomed to the immediacy of Twitter and Snapchat. Individual voices get marginalized and buried and drowned by the tidal wave of trendy babel, nonsense and noise. Imagine the likes of a Jack Kerouac today. He'd never happen. One must first be commodity, marketed, and then perhaps later touted as a genius. This is the by-product of the global consumerism and information age. There's so much out there, too much of everything, and in order to remain reasonably intact and sane, one must shut down, block out and ignore. We're all filters now, and most of us aren't really present, no, we're on our phones. There, not there. The phone is an extension of us as walking filters, unwilling to confront our neighbor or a stranger, living by the techno-driven rule that to survive is to push away, to close the mind, to shut down, to delete. We never see another's discerning eyes when we lash out in a heated overly emotional text, our language chosen poorly.

Sometimes, I think that only an idiot asking for a beatdown walks around with eyes, ears and heart open. Well, maybe not an idiot. Let's call that person a child. Of course, childhood ends now much sooner than it used to. By the age of five, most kids are getting programmed, stamped, shaped into cruel arbiters of so-called taste and erudition. The right schools, the right clothes, the brand name products, and the phone. Can't go anywhere without your

Apple or your Android because it's the new sense of home.

I learned that Waldsmith once owned his own book-store, had sold thousands of volumes in his day. As a pub-lished author, he hadn't left a novel for the world to carry, but rather he'd become a leading authority on stereoscope cards, describing the old stereoscope viewers to my wife, who, thanks to my interest in such arcana, knew a little bit about what they were. I mentioned Carleton Watkins and how he was one of my favorite photographers of the American West and had shot photos for such cards. Mr. Waldsmith brightened upon hearing this, saying of course he knew about Watkins, but regrettably he didn't have any cards by him.

He started telling me that what he called his "best specimens" of stereoscope cards were still at his home. Yes, home is where you keep your valued objects. Wald-smith was in the process of liquidating his collections and, apparently, he had many stereoscope cards, quite an ex-tensive amount. He was speaking to us now in a more sincere manner, without trying to sell us, having shucked off his forced Midwestern friendliness. He sounded bitter as he told us he'd sold off nearly all his valuable books and was "getting out, selling off everything." He'd had his fill of "the business."

Before we could ask him why, he said, "Alzheimer's." It was getting worse. The pain of knowing he'd been a thinker and an "archivist and a collector" all his life and now being unable to remember the simplest of things, without any logic to the deep memory loss, without any control over his mind, though he was only in his mid-60s, was too much to bear. Some days were better than others. He couldn't handle the work any longer. Some days he couldn't even remember his own name. Thank God for his wife, who wasn't with him that day, but she was helping him sell off his store on the Internet. He was afraid of what might happen next. An ordeal both terrible and horrific. "What can I do?" he asked. "Nothing."

My wife, who works with dementia patients as an occupational therapist, showed a visible twinge of pain in her usually placid face. I felt my own face reddening. A light rain had begun to fall and the few brave dealers who'd laid out tarps and blankets in the parking lot began to gather their goods and load them back into vans. Luckily, we were under a roof and though it was cold and damp it was tolerable. Learning this about Mr. Waldsmith, however, had lowered the heat, so to speak, and made it more difficult, at least for me, to enjoy his companionship. I felt too much pity. I couldn't help myself. He just wasn't that old, but without question, by his own admission, his life as he knew it was entering a final phase, one that might have him withering on the vine in a state of helplessness for many years to come. I remember my late mother once remarking, "Sometimes, it's a blessing to go quick."

He said he didn't want to wallow in self-pity. Looking at him, his nose so pink with cold, his eyes rheumy, wandering and unable to meet my gaze, I felt an overwhelming sense of grief. I wished that money could help him in some way, but I knew better. I had enough cash in my pocket to buy about $50 worth of his postage stamps, many of them from Egypt, but that was my road money for a long drive back from Ohio to Virginia. Besides, such a purchase really wouldn't have changed his fate, his disease, the complete vanishing of his calling as an archivist. How, I wondered, had he felt when seeing the Internet replace him? Then to see his faculties deteriorate, and to watch this continue daily while putting on a show of living a normal life? I couldn't think of anything worse than seeing one's own demise happen in stages, inexorably, and having no means to stop it.

It was much to process given the dampness and chilly early hour and the long drive I had ahead of me. The impending rain had come, and now the sky's ashen color and a sudden dip in the temperature presaged snow. We had to hit the road. Our visit to Ohio was ending, unfortunately, whether we wanted it to or not.

I wrote down Waldsmith's name, hoping that by taking this information it might comfort him. At the time, I wasn't much younger than he was, maybe ten years or so. I promised him I'd look up his book on line. He told me not to buy the first edition, since the pricings on the stereoscope cards were out of date. I should get the second edition when available and I should understand that it was the "definitive" book on the subject. He could not stress this enough. See, his book, his passion, was a form of home and he wanted me to be his guest.

A few months later, while browsing in an antique mall, something we're likely to do as a couple during a Sunday drive to nowhere, I came across a copy of Waldsmith's book. I'd forgotten about him. For all I knew, he'd died or been hospitalized. It was a new copy. Unlike Waldsmith himself, it shined. I got lost in it standing there in that mall, unbothered, and I learned about stereoscope cards, their general history, as well as capsulized histories of various images, their photographers, when the images were taken, all sorts of interesting tidbits, each image thoroughly researched and presented with a reason for it to be considered important or valuable on the collector market.

I found this more than small comfort, realizing Mr. Waldsmith would go into complete oblivion soon, up there in northern Ohio, if he hadn't passed into that realm already. His book, his sense of home mattered, at least to me, as proof that the man had made a positive mark. He'd changed me. Deepened me. And not just for money, but out of passion and a need to comfort and guide others. There had to be other wanderers out there, just like me, with a burning interest in these old cards who'd used Waldsmith's book as an encyclopedia. How many such books existed on this topic? I ventured to think very few, if any. Perhaps Mr. Waldsmith had been right. Perhaps he really was the leading scholar on this topic, but to think that the man might live into his 80s, for another 15 to 20 years, and need constant care and attention, felt ghastly, really, to accept. Coupled with this was the thought that he had perhaps already forgotten all he'd learned and written, not only about stereoscope cards, but everything.

Years later while in Turkey, where I currently live, I learned about Brian May, the former guitarist for Queen who now has a PhD in astrophysics from Imperial College London, and his mania for all things parallax via stereoscope cards. May started collecting these cards as a boy using a Weetabix 3-D Viewer. He's gone on to write a number of books on the subject, including *Queen In 3-D*, in which stereoscope pictures taken by him with a stereo 3-D camera, detail pieces of the life of that massively successful band. As a rock musician always on the road, May's lifelong fascination with stereoscope cards supports my definition of home. It's not one place. It's a consistent sense of pleasure and a welcoming reassurance when one gets lost in the doing, the venturing. What May and Waldsmith find in their cards is the home I find between an old book's pages. Is it possible that to be home is to feel a thrilling sense of embarking toward someplace new? I believe so.

I wish Brian May could meet John Waldsmith. That will never happen, of course. I often remember Waldsmith out in that open air, the cold wind nipping at his extremities, selling dank dissolving remains from what was once a prized treasure trove, a living museum, a life's work and passion. It was as if he was being buried alive and it was all so thoroughly unkind.

The Accident House

Debra Frank

Screech of brakes, crunch of metal on metal, squealing tires, broken parts clattering along the road: the house I lived in with my father when I was 13 to 15 had a soundtrack. Whenever I heard it, I shuddered, tossed my book down, and dashed to the kitchen, where I grabbed the wall phone receiver as I pulled back the curtains to assess the damage.

Most of the accidents run together in my memory: cars at odd angles, splinters of glass and metal, dents and scrapes, people hunched on the ground, heads in hands. It was the different ways people coped that intrigued me. Some sobbed as though it was the end of the world, some froze, and some jumped out of their cars, completed the reports, and moved on. It didn't seem to matter how bad the accident itself was.

In one of the first, a light blue Volkswagen bug had spun on to the gravel and patchy grass of our side yard, while across the road, a tan El Dorado with a dented fender faced the wrong direction up hill. The people emerging from the vehicles didn't look injured, but I dialed 911, knowing by then the dispatcher would send the police to sort things out.

After supplying my name and address and hanging up, I poured a couple glasses of water and went outside to the patchy clouds of a warm July day. It made me feel important to help. These people were having a bad day, and I fancied myself as a welcoming committee of sorts. I thought I ought to keep folding chairs on hand, but my father would never have sprung for that.

A lady in her thirties, swathed in dark curls, was seated on our grass, wailing. The man she was with knelt by her, and tried to put his arm around her, but she shook him off. "I can't, I can't, I can't," she said between sobs, though her car didn't look that bad, a shattered headlamp and some scrapes. I handed her a glass and told her the police were on their way—which made her wail louder. I hurried off to get tissues.

A half hour later you would never guess there'd just been an accident. As always, the broken cars were gone, the glittering glass swept away, the site restored to clean concrete and tufts of grass, barely flattened. A single call, and the rescuers came—at minimum the police, but sometimes an ambulance, fire truck, and even a tow truck.

It wasn't that simple for me. Every crash I heard at the Accident House—as we'd begun to call it after seven accidents in two months—went through my body like a cymbal clash, reverberating with remembered danger, and the sadness, and self-doubt that followed. The year before, I'd needed to be rescued, but I hadn't known who to call, or how to ask for help.

My parents divorced when I was nine, and up until the last couple months, I'd lived with my mother. She'd always had boyfriends, but they left early in the morning and had their own homes to return to. Not Clyde. He didn't so much arrive as land in our home, wearing nearly everything he owned—baggy shorts and a button-down shirt worn open over his Rolling Stones t-shirt, the one with the big tongue. I met him on the day he moved in. I was twelve.

He seemed affable enough, that first evening. He cooked us sopapillas, deep fried dough that puffed into delicious crispy pillows. Then he'd suggested a walk, which was nice until he wanted to hold my hand. That seemed odd to me.

But within a few weeks, I hated everything about Clyde. His ruddy face that squished up when he laughed. The long coils of rust-colored hair. The way his sandals slapped the floor. His whistling that said I don't have a care in the world. The stink of his Camels and the pungent wispy plumes coming from his thin-papered joints. The way he spent my mother's scant income so there was nothing left for groceries, and sometimes not enough to keep the heat on and the water running.

But I hated most the way he waited naked by the front door, so I'd have to pass in front of him when I came home from school or my babysitting job. When I would look away and hurry past, he would call out, *Hey! Haven't you seen a naked man before?*

My mother took up Clyde's cause. I found her in the kitchen one afternoon where I'd gone to search the empty cupboards and fridge. She wore her usual beige cardigan, and the tomato-red pants she'd stolen from a laundromat a few years earlier. At 36, she was pale and plump, her waist-length black hair gone gray, but still billowy, her crowning glory, she always said. How she kept on the extra weight made me wonder. I used my babysitting money to buy school lunch, and I had meals with my father on Sundays during his parenting time, but that was it. Was my mother hiding food for her and Clyde, while I went without?

But she had something other than food on her mind. She dipped her tea bag into her mug and set it aside. Then, without further preamble, she said, "Clyde needs sex at least twice every day." She giggled, large brown eyes sparkling, as if we were schoolgirls sharing confidences. "And he believes," she added, "that it's the duty of the man of the house to teach the young girls about sex."

I gaped at her, reluctant to connect her two statements. But her next question seemed to complete her trifecta, "So, have you done *It* yet?"

I backed out of the kitchen, away from her, into my bedroom, closing my door as if that made me safe. If she'd come right out and said, "Clyde wants to have sex with you and I think that's grand because twice a day is too much for me," I'd have been horrified. And yet if I'd connected the dots, that's exactly what she'd said. I took refuge in my bedroom and tucked my fear away as best I could where it festered, unnamed, and became a low-throttled humming thing, something that might rupture or blow up if nudged. Years later I would learn my mother was an incest victim. She must have been conditioned to say yes to predatory men, drawing them to her, like the scent of blood draws ambulance chasers.

My mother didn't bring it up again, but for nine famished months, I kept my bedroom door shut and hoped for the best. I never asked for help—there was no 911 for a malnourished twelve-year-old living in fear of her mother's boyfriend. No dispatcher to ask the nature of my emergency. No one to send food. No one to haul Clyde away.

My fears about Clyde ended when, to my surprise,

he removed himself and took my mother with him. He'd decided it was time to work again, after a year's break, and he and my mother found a studio suitable for him to teach ballroom dancing—or *touch dancing* as he always called it. They moved there, saying it was too small to take me—to my relief. I stayed where I was, still hungry but safe from Clyde, and wondered how many rent payments they would make, if any.

My father had a series of girlfriends after the divorce, all dark-haired, brown-eyed, pretty, each lasting about a year, or about the amount of time it took them to realize he had no intention of marrying again. I liked all of them in their turn. They came along on our Sunday excursions to the movies or a mall, to the Seattle Center rides, or hiking on Mt. Rainier. Beth was my father's girlfriend during the Clyde year.

One Sunday, we were driving toward Rainier, and I was prattling on about planets, or the light spectrum, or whatever I'd recently learned from my weekly stack of library books, when Beth gave out an exasperated sigh and said something that sounded like, "know-it-all" under her breath. I clammed up immediately. I was a shy, quiet kid, but I could be chatty when I found an audience. At home I'd wanted to disappear because it was dangerous to be in a young female body, but otherwise I ached to be seen, acknowledged, cared for.

I may have irritated Beth, but it was she who realized something wasn't right. I was thin, ragged, agitated, and I ate ravenously if given the chance, but if anyone noticed, they hadn't said. Beth did. She came to my rescue by urging my father to talk to me. When he asked, "Is there anything you want to tell me?" I sputtered, cried, and finally poured out the whole story. My father gave me grocery money until he found a rental house for us to move into.

The house was a spacious brick ranch, its wood siding painted a salmon color, on a corner lot, on a street where people took care of their lawns and planted flowers. It was solid and conventional, clean, and well-maintained, with sliding glass doors to a deck facing the back yard and large windows in front which seemed to keep watch on all those crashes. Only its location was precarious—on a residential street caught between two commercial zones. Cars speeding down the hill toward our intersection, away from the mall and strip centers above, and toward the car lots and fast food restaurants below, collided with inattentive drivers on our residential side street as they drifted through the yield signs.

The Accident House was back in my old neighborhood, where we'd lived before the divorce. That meant I was once again among kids I hadn't seen for the three years since I'd moved away. I'd stayed in touch with my grade school best friend, Janet, but when I told her I was coming back to the neighborhood, she warned, "My friends are really picky," pausing for several seconds before adding, "but I'm sure you'll be fine."

I spotted her on the first day of school, standing with several girls I didn't know, pretty girls with a practiced nonchalance, a way of laughing on cue while keeping track of the traffic around them with a discreet eye. They had flipped hair, flared jeans, and frosty eyeshadow in blues and purples. Oblivious of my unflipped hair, my barely-there mascara, my unbranded jeans, I called, "Hi!" to Janet, but she looked slightly alarmed and turned in a few degrees more, as if closing a gate. Apparently, I was not "fine."

After my mother left, I hadn't thought I would see her again. But she called sometimes. In February, eight months after I'd moved in with my father, she asked me to join her at the Seattle Center for a cat show. As we strolled the aisles looking at the pretty creatures in cages, she told me she'd had an abortion not long after the divorce. She said, "That's water under the bridge now, but Clyde and I are thinking about having a baby." I suppressed a grimace.

My mother didn't like me to be so quiet. "You know, you really need to talk about your feelings more," she said. "It's not good to keep them bottled up inside." The cat show cages made me feel tired. Behind bars, the cats couldn't cuddle. They weren't there as pets but for display, to be judged on such things as the size of their ears, the width versus length of their heads, how tapered their tails were. How many kittens hadn't measured up? How many had been discarded?

Coming back from the cat show, the bus let me off a couple blocks from the Accident House. In the slanting rain, I had to cross a five-lane thoroughfare. My light was green, so I started across, but then I saw the dark hull of a left-turning car coming at me. No time to dodge it—I was knocked to the street. I got up soaked but without difficulty, just a few scrapes, and scurried back to the curb. The driver pulled over and rolled down his window. "I'm so sorry! Are you okay?"

"Yes, fine," I said, but he asked a few more times before driving away slowly. At home, I shut myself in my room and for the first time since moving there, I sobbed. The driver wanted to help me, and I wished he could have—but my hurt didn't come from him.

Shortly after the cat show, still feeling despondent, I

looked out my window, where we had a seven-foot circle of dead grass from the most memorable accident. It had happened several weeks after we moved in. I'd heard the usual crash followed by an especially loud thump, an impact that made the house shudder. Outside my bedroom window, I saw a white van upside down in our front yard, directly in front of me, having sailed over a three-foot berm. As I watched, a blond man wearing white painter's pants eased out of the driver-side window, patted his thighs as if brushing something off—and then walked over to the other car without so much as a limp.

The elderly couple in the other car, a green sedan spun around to face the wrong way, did not get out. I watched the blond man trying to communicate with them, but they seemed paralyzed. Most people got out of their cars quickly and walked around looking at the damage. They might not like what they saw, but at least they looked. When a police officer arrived, he had to knock on the window before those people got out.

Later, a tow truck had come and yanked the van right side up and hauled it away. Then a pair of firemen had sprayed their hoses at the matted grass.

Now, looking at the dead grass from months earlier, I thought about the man in painter's pants and how calm he'd been. Probably he had a new car now and had forgotten about the crash. Or maybe he laughed about it. Or even bragged about it. His was the most dramatic accident—and he'd shown the least dramatic reaction. It gave me a thought about the emptiness I felt. Maybe I could see it as a blank canvas, a new beginning.

When my mother called again, I told her, "No, I'd rather not." She protested, but each time I stood my ground, I felt stronger. At school, most of the kids didn't know me, so I had a chance with them. I summoned my courage and *pretended* to be confident and pretty—it helped to discover curling irons and eye shadow—and I sent this facsimile of myself out to the classrooms, hallways, and cafeteria of my junior high. Somehow it worked. I fooled people. I collected friends and I stopped caring that Janet wasn't one of them.

My father and I lived at the Accident House for just two years, but they were important ones for me. *Take your pick,* the house seemed to say. *You can sob on the side of the road, or you can accept the hard knocks and get on with your life.*

I still think of the Accident House whenever I hear a loud noise. Those crashes were woven into my memories of the preceding Clyde year, like aftershocks. Now when someone drops a pan, the wind slams a door, or the dog barks sharply at a delivery person I feel a heart-stopping stab of fear. For a moment, life is dangerous again, and I'm paralyzed. Then it passes, and I'm reminded that even a real emergency isn't likely to be the end of the world.

On a recent visit back to Seattle, decades later, I was sad when I discovered the Accident House was no longer watching over its corner. The commercial strip below had blown out of its boundaries and crept up the hill, taking out the house, and a few of its neighbors. I didn't like the look of the black and blue building that took its place, it was too big and imposing, it didn't blend with the landscape like the Accident House did. And what exactly was it? I had to circle around another time to see. A storage locker business. A place to put the stuff you're holding on to.

Inheritance

Karin Hedetniemi

Summer of '74

Grandma has a half-acre with a small, gnarly apple orchard where fallen apples rot sweet and pungent in the heat. I like to climb the trees and peer back toward her house. There's a weathered tool shed stuffed with old clay pots, a lawn-mower, rakes, galvanized buckets of wooden laundry pins, a rolled-up hammock, and my grandfather's hand tools. I never met my grandfather. He died when my mother was still in school. The tool shed smells earthy, musty, a mix of gasoline and age. Grandma is around the back, where the sun reaches all day. She's staking tomatoes and tying string for sugar peas. She looks happy.

23 years, Tending

When she emptied out the tool shed, the old hammock had disintegrated. *Squirrels probably used it for nesting material. I'm sorry, honey.* My boys are giggling inside their treehouse, slapping playing cards on the wooden floor.

They've thrown their raggedy, half-chewed pea pods in the grass, abandoned with metal trucks and dusty sneakers. In summer, they are wild and free. I stomp to flatten the cardboard, clip the shiny S-hooks to the poles, and stretch out in the quilt of my grandmother's generosity. It fills me with an unidentified longing, a fleeting nostalgia, tiny minnows nibbling my skin.

11 years, Potential

The neighbor is telling me there used to be an extensive vegetable garden in the backyard. "Too bad the house flipper covered it with sod. To appeal to more buyers, I guess. Not everyone wants to take care of a big garden. But that's got to be amazing soil. You could restart a veggie patch, you know. By the way, that tree is probably eighty years old. Gravenstein, a heritage apple." My husband is at the far end of the property, head tilted back, frozen in mid-step by a bewitching bird call. I silently approach the elder tree. It has one precariously leaning arm, propped up by a plank that long ago became fused. I put my hands gently on the bark, test my footing in the V of its trunk. It feels sturdy.

8 years, Solace

At 10:25 am, the July sun is already hot enough. I drift through the garden, reconnecting with plants tended long ago in another world, letting sunlight stream into the rooms of my heart. The first of summer apples have fallen in long grass. I find a galvanized pail and collect them for the neighbor. She's always making pies. I drag rusty poles out on the lawn to set up the hammock and collapse into the gentle sway, a tender cupping of my soul. Sleep comes as little laps onshore. From somewhere in the cedars, the resident wren dispatches his distinctive buzzy call. My husband doesn't hear it. He died three hours ago.

3 years, Renewal

At 10:25 am, the foghorns are still going. I open the gate. No one's been here for a while. A hummingbird chirps sharply from behind the lilac bush: *This is my yard.* Grapevines stretch upward from the arbor, seeking heat. I can smell a salty sea breeze, rushing across the leaves. The yard is compact, with overgrown garden beds, a fallen fence, an old brick patio, and a newly constructed tool shed, vacant except for a pegboard and a sun-bleached guide to growing herbs. There is plenty of room to store the hammock over winter. I find a galvanized watering can and give the tomato plants a drink. They are thirsty for summer, like me.

2 Rms, Family View:
The Ones We Call Home

Anndee Hochman

Three days after James moved in, we left him on his own in the house for the weekend. The ink was barely dry on our closing papers; we were still unpacking the 65 boxes of books we'd schlepped from Portland, Oregon.

We needed a housemate to occupy the third floor of our new home, a Victorian single in Northwest Philadelphia—and, not incidentally, to help foot the mortgage. James was a third-year law student—too polite and congenial, we figured, to be a serial killer.

Still, we were nervous. Would this stranger leave a potholder too close to the gas flame? Forget to lock the security door? Would our computers still be there when we returned? Would he?

We opened the door on Sunday afternoon to a waft of chocolate and butter. A plate of warm cookies sat on the counter. And there was James, paging through *Sundays at Moosewood Restaurant* and deciding what to make for dinner.

It's been 20 years, and as many housemates, since then.

We thumbtack notes to the food co-op bulletin board or post on Craigslist: "Seeking friendly, flexible person to share our home." We used to describe ourselves as "lesbian couple with a feisty toddler and two affectionate cats." Later we added "tofu-loving hamster" to the mix. Now we call Sasha an "energetic adolescent"; we've become "midlife moms." The tofu-loving hamster, sadly, is buried near the blueberry bush.

Housemate-hunting is a little like online dating, except the stakes are so much higher. We're not just choosing someone to meet for Cosmos in a public place; this stranger will, within days of our first meeting, carry keys to our house and memorize the code to our security alarm. He'll hear us argue. She'll know the sound of an energetic adolescent who is furious at her midlife moms, a bedroom door slammed loud enough to hurt your teeth.

In this intimate setting, none of us can hide our quirks for long. We'll soon learn that one housemate can't remember to close a cabinet door. Another eats a toasted English muffin for breakfast every single morning. A third fields late-night phone calls from her unreliable, alcoholic ex.

We've become adept at vetting responses to our ads, sorting the merely neurotic from the flat-out nuts. We reject anyone whose note screams: "NEED PLACE IMMEDIATELY SAFE NEIGHBORHOOD PREFER SMALL SECURITY DEPOSIT." We've learned the code: "home-based entrepreneur" means "I have no job," and someone who self-describes as "itinerant" might not stay past the next season.

Others make it over the e-mail hurdle only to prove incompatible on sight: The woman with chemical sensitivities who sniffed inside the closet and grimaced at the Windex bottle beneath the kitchen sink. The man who sighed after touring the third floor and said, "I know myself, and I just can't live in a room with sloped ceilings." The one who talked nonstop for twenty minutes—her crazy boss, her troubled adult daughter—after we asked, "Can you tell us a little about yourself?"

Sometimes we've gone without rent for a month or two while waiting for the right person to come along. And just when we start to feel despondent, there they are: a disarming e-mail with a splash of sardonic humor; a phone call from someone who sounds warm and kind.

Housemates often come to us in transition: bruised from a bad relationship, recently downsized at work, in flight from parental demands, in search of a soft landing. We've shared our home with a college administrator, a staff artist for a natural-foods market, a digital animator, a bilingual anthropologist, a computer software engineer, a transgender playwright, several rabbinical students and a pair of circus artists who specialized in duo trapeze.

They live with us for a summer, or six months, or five years. Our lives intertwine: a little, a lot. James made an elaborate house dinner nearly every Sunday. Anthony knelt with us by a bedroom window to gape at the lunar eclipse. Munish helped Sasha, then four, make a city out of shoeboxes. Housemates have fed our hyperthyroid cat while we're away; in turn, we've watered their spider plants.

In twenty years, only one person left owing us money.

Mostly, they depart beneficently: Jamie gave us her Cuisinart blender, which Victoria (two housemates later) used every morning to make an algae-colored smoothie with kale, blueberries and almond milk. MJ planted beets and basil in the back yard. There are items on the third floor whose provenance we can't place: a lime-green winter jacket, an extra vacuum, a mysterious roll of beige felt.

But our housemates' legacy goes beyond the tangible. They nudge us out of the insular bubble that a small nuclear family can become. They people our lives with difference; they expand the envelope of conversation. From Ann, we learned about Peruvian textiles; with MJ, we talked playwriting. Megan practiced handstands in the living room and figured out how to unfreeze the bathtub pipes. Sometimes, they become good friends.

We've attended former housemates' weddings and baby showers; with others, even years later, we trade e-mail updates and occasional photos. A few, though, just vanished. What happened to Judah, who never did learn to sort the recyclables from the trash? Did Deb get sober and go to graduate school? And what about Ari, divorced with a two-year-old, who moved out after she was laid off from the vegan bakery? I hope she found a gentle place to land.

"Aren't you worried about having housemates, with a kid?" people ask, and I know they're thinking about pedophiles and sociopaths. All I can say is that we rely on self-selection, intuition, references...and no small amount of luck.

My partner and her brothers grew up in a rambling Denver house that welcomed a series of live-in graduate and exchange students; my childhood home always had an open door and a spare bed for a cousin or friend in need. So this is our normal: extra sets of keys jangling on the rack, someone else's music filtering through our bedroom ceiling, the soft beep-beep of a housemate coming home late, setting the alarm and padding up two flights of wooden steps.

What will our daughter make of this shifting cast of characters? Maybe the thing my partner and I have long believed: Most people are good. All of us are flawed. Home isn't a hash-mark on a map, but a nexus of experiences, a slow accretion of Shabbat dinners and slammed doors, game nights and birthday cakes, relationships sundered and others knit for a lifetime. A skinny Victorian house can be a spacious refuge. And strangers are just the people you haven't yet gotten to know.

When Sasha was six, and our third floor temporarily vacant, she slipped upstairs with a silver Sharpie and inked the names of our housemates onto a corner of the blond wood: James, Grace, Cynthia, Charley, Munish, Deb, Judah...

We made her erase it with fine-grade sandpaper. But her touch was light, maybe on purpose, and the names didn't completely disappear. If you squint, in the late afternoon when amber light spills through the dormers, you can still see them, all the people who left their indelible print on our lives.

Cornwall Village: "A Remembrancer Designedly Dropt"

Richard Holinger

"A child said, What is the grass? fetching it to me with full hands...
I guess it is the handkerchief of the Lord,
A scented gift and remembrancer designedly dropt."

—Walt Whitman, *Song of Myself*, Section 6

The one square block of Cornwall Village, an hour's drive northwest of Hartford, set above Coltsfoot Valley's long, green meadow, might be God's handkerchief, dropped to remind us what beauty and tranquility can be found in a small rural Connecticut town. Returning fifty-two years after graduating from The Marvelwood School, and writing about it now, I can make that comparison, seeing—and feeling—its halcyon beauty.

Which was nothing like the psychological thunderstorm raging when, at thirteen-years-old, I said goodbye to my mother in Chicago's Union Station five decades ago.

Sitting up in a coach seat overnight, all I had to think about was how much I would miss my luxury Lake Shore Drive apartment with parking attendants, uniformed doormen, part-time laundress, and live-in cook and cat; my friends from the elementary, grade, and middle school I cherished from Junior Kindergarten; weekends exploring the woods and ravines surrounding the private Pullman mansion on rails my grandfather bought when it was retired in 1935, perched above Rock Creek's slow carp and turtle-filled waters outside Plano, Illinois (yes, the tackle box town).

Arriving in New York, I carried my two suitcases through Grand Central Station until someone from the school made himself known. We vanned north for two hours before turning south off Route 4 and entered Cornwall Village from where I wouldn't leave until mid-December, for Christmas vacation. After checking in with the M.O.D. (Master of the Day), I was assigned a room in Rumsey Hall, its exterior Greek columns and bold Colonial façade masking its interior rooms with endless ceilings, fissured walls, and splintery wooden floors.

My return to Cornwall more than a half a century later found everything changed and nothing changed.

"Where do you want to go first?" my wife, Tia, asked as she, my daughter Molly, and I turned off Route 4, civilization left behind completely as if entering a magic wardrobe or The Shire. A sunny somnambulance enveloped Molly's Camry like a benign fog. Tia and I had flown from our home in Geneva, Illinois, an hour west of Chicago, where we both taught in parochial secondary schools, to see Molly, a doctoral student in Creative Studies at University of Connecticut. It was mid-July. The trees billowed green and full above us as we crept past where Calhoun

House, my junior year dorm, surely stood, although time and memory hid it from me.

"There's a historical society." Tia pointed to a sign in front of a typical Cornwall house. If she'd indicated pterodactyl roadkill, I couldn't have been more disbelieving. An historical society? For Cornwall?

"I need to go to the bathroom," I said, my mantra at 70-years-old. "Let's see if the library's open."

We parked across the street, feeling fairly safe from being ticketed (in my four years as a preppie in town, I never saw a police car or officer). *Although closed, the library offered a partial peek into the auditorium where I once played a guard in Shakespeare's* Henry IV. *The director, most likely an English teacher, encouraged me, for the sake of verisimilitude, to remove my glasses before going onstage, leaving me gasping not only orally when delivering my one or two lines, but visually as well. More successful was the variety show night my freshman roommate Bob Lamb and I did impressions of ABC's Harry Reasoner and Howard K. Smith reporting faux news.*

"Maybe we should start at the historical society," Tia suggested, the idea of a toilet inside more an incentive for me than reviewing the past. We walked back through the 85-degree afternoon, umbrellaed from the sun by occasional trees to the air-conditioned house where a young volunteer behind a small desk welcomed us. I told the man I was a Marvelwood graduate, a fact that brought a smile both polite and pitying, as if I'd confessed to him that I'd never had my bunions removed.

The largest display, a wall full of photos, chronologically unfolded the July 10, 1989, tornado that ripped up many of Coltsfoot Valley's Cathedral Pines. Coincidentally, leaving at 1:00 p.m. today, the museum offered a "30ᵗʰ Anniversary Hike in Cathedral Pines." Not that I would have signed on if the group hadn't already departed, but it felt like we'd arrived in town on a holy day everyone else had remembered and prepared for.

Strolling back to the welcome desk, I asked the docent, "Is Rumsey still there?" in the same manner a swimmer might ask a lifeguard, "Is the shark still offshore?"

"No," he said, noticeably sad, which meant he'd never boarded there. "The tornado took off part of Rumsey Hall's roof. In 2010, the village decided to demolish it."

"Thank God!" I blurted, unable to control my ecstasy, turbulent memories still clear, nightmares returning often.

One such recurring dream manifested from a Saturday night after the cafeteria movie and thrilling pulp fiction chapter from "The Spider's Web" (...on speckled black and white film, a fancy 1930's Dodge racing along a dark night road [cut to] a speeding train headed toward certain disaster unless [cut to] The Spider, in close-up, face wrapped in what looks like a black sheet covered with white tic-tac-toe games, can stop it). Returning that night to the dorm, I opened my door, flicked on the light, and saw a rat, seemingly the size of a cougar, scurry across the room, leaving a blond potato chip trail to his escape route, down a radiator pipe's hole. He had bored a hole into the bag beneath which broken, golden nuggets pooled. I stuffed the hole with towels and later lay in bed, in the dark, unable to move, unable to sleep, listening for the rat's return, an image that haunted me long after leaving Cornwall.

Next morning, when I told the teacher in charge of my dorm wing, he scoffed, "That's what you get for having food in your room."

The single positive attribute Rumsey's age offered was its creaky floors, an alarm that seniors or masters stalked the hall, giving us time to shut up or ditch whatever we were reading instead of solving geometry problems or an English paper. Only once was permission to leave our rooms from the 7:20 to 9:50 study hall hours granted, the night we gathered in the building's main hall, bare and echoing, to watch the Fab Four perform before screaming girls on The Ed Sullivan Show *in blurry shades of gray.*

On the way out, I picked up the museum's free brochures and stopped to read Mark van Doran's "The Little Hills of Cornwall," the poem spelled out on the wall behind the welcome desk. In my journal, written later that day, I critiqued the verse as "trite and silly," but I'd just skimmed the wall rendering. When I Google it now and read it more slowly, its personification still cloys, but my initial review seems reductive:

> The hills of little Cornwall
> Themselves are dreams.
> The mind lies down among them,
> Even by day, and snores,
> Snug in the perilous knowledge
> That nothing more inward pleasing,
> More like itself,
> Sleeps anywhere beyond them
> Even by night
> In the great land it cares two pins about,
> Possibly; not more.
>
> The mind, eager for caresses,
> Lies down at its own risk in Cornwall;
> Whose hills, Whose cunning streams,
> Whose mazes where a thought,

Doubling upon itself,
Considers the way, lazily, well lost,
Indulge it to the nick of death—
Not quite, for where it curls it still can feel,
Like feathers,
Like affectionate mouse whiskers,
he flattery, the trap.

The poem channels Eliot's cat curling about the house in "Prufrock," or maybe Sandburg's "little cat feet" in "Fog." But one still wonders how the author of this poem could have influenced the likes of Berryman, Ginsberg, Kerouac, and Merton.

As we left the museum and walked back to the car, Tia asked if I wanted to walk around the town's one main block or drive. "Let's drive," I said, *unable to repeat one more time those thousands of perambulations from dorm(s) to dining room and classroom buildings under blazing hot suns, harsh cloudbursts, and frigid snowstorms. Occasionally we were sent back to collect forgotten texts or homework during the class day, English teacher Ed Sundt directing profligates, "On your horse!"*

Driving leisurely as Dickinson's coach driver Death, we passed the Congregational Church or, as listed in the historical brochure, the United Church of Christ. *In that puritanically bare interior, the school gathered on Sunday late afternoons for Vespers, a non-denominational service in which guest speakers tried to keep us from spending the forty-five minutes entertaining ourselves by farting and giggling. The one orator I remember from four years of pew sitting, a prison chaplain, had us at, "I'm not so good with names, but I'm a whizz at numbers."*

Next door, or what used to be next door, a flat, unmown, grassy plot was all that marked where Rumsey Hall once stood. Glee filled me as we glided past, as though Tough the Bully had finally gotten his due, or the Wicked Witch of the West had melted into obscurity.

"Do you want to take a picture?" Tia asked.

No, I didn't. *Too many pictures remained in my mind: the rat, of course, but also the communal non-draining soapy basement shower stall, the non-partitioned toilets, the bony, uncarpeted floors. Historical significance be damned; this building, like the Confederacy, did not deserve remembrance.*

On the afternoon of November 22 of my freshman year, as I rode my bike from Rumsey back to afternoon classes, a passing student called out, "Kennedy's been shot!" As monumental the news was everywhere else, hitting the world like an errant meteor, its impact on Cornwall, sequestered from the world, mattered little. Getting to class on time, getting the homework done, getting through soccer practice—or was it the beginning of hockey season?— took precedence.

We drove past the grassy clearing where a brown path, thin as the tundra hairline trail taken by Jack London's *chechoquo*, cut across to the campus center. To our left, the practice field still stood *where our bespectacled, British-born soccer coach once yelled, "It's the SNAP of the knee!" With a population of only ninety-two students, the school encouraged everyone to go out for sports; I spent four years as a fullback toe-kicking goal kicks, my big toe after practices and games bloody and raw.*

Another left turn brought us to the barn that once housed our dining room, assembly hall, and miniature basketball court. Today, the museum docent had told us, it was a private residence. Stately brick Calhoun House now held two artists and their studio. In Spring, 1963, Calhoun functioned as dorm, classroom building, and administrative center. *My mother and I had sat across the desk from Bob Bodkin, the school's founder and headmaster, who told us he'd take me as long as I went to Maine's Winter Harbor Reading Camp that summer.*

I did learn how to read in that rambling seacoast house where bunk beds allowed rooms for four to six other non-readers, and where every morning I'd vomit before breakfast from homesickness. Taught to read actively (skim, read/underline, review), I pass on that wisdom to my high school students today. However, as well as the camp taught me how to read, it didn't make me enjoy reading. That enlightenment came later, at Marvelwood, but not in a classroom.

One day, my roommate, Bob Lamb, reading a novel in a comfy chair he'd brought from home, asked, "Hey, how come you never read anything?"

Lamb had a knack for asking impertinent, aggressive questions that suggested there was something wrong with me. I don't know how I answered, but I'm sure his tone pissed me off, so I probably offered up something witty like, "Why do you care?"

"Here," he said, throwing a paperback at me. "Read this."

I looked at the title. The Arrangement, by Elia Kazan. I started reading it, and something happened. I became absorbed in the story. I cared about the characters and their world. I was reading satire. I was reading about rebellion from the expected, routine, suburban middle-class life.

If Bob hadn't thrown me that book, I might be rich,

but stressed out, might be donning a dark business suit, starchy white-collared shirt and monochrome tie every day, and carrying cost-ratio figures or legal renderings in a monogrammed leather briefcase. Instead, I've spent forty-plus years teaching high school English with a smattering of years as a night-class community college adjunct instructor. When not preparing lesson plans, grading papers, or responding to emails, I'm writing a column for a local paper, facilitating a creative writing group, or writing the occasional essay, poem, or short story.

Winter Harbor's reading skills helped my freshman grades, although not as much as Marvelwood's emphasis on study skills and time management. Assignment planners, proctored study halls, small class sizes, individuated learning, and teachers' close scrutiny of reading and homework assignments all contributed to my success in college (Hartwick), a Master's in English (Washington University), and a doctorate in Creative Writing (University of Illinois at Chicago). Bob Bodkin's dream of taking a kid with unused potential was realized in me, among hundreds of others.

Now, to our right, Coltsfoot Valley looked just as lush and serene as remembered. *While attending school, I didn't see it for its Emersonian Transcendental joy, never experienced his "transparent eyeball" at one with forest, meadow, and brook. Instead, my homesick adolescence merely gazed on the idyllic scene apart from it, longing to be somewhere other than where cows grazed, and firs swayed. Feeling locked within a rural dystopia, escape for me only over the two major holidays, Christmas and Easter, flying from Bradley Field to O'Hare, I cried every time returning home when an older brother or parent stood waiting for me at Arrivals.*

We drove down the narrow valley road *where once I pedaled a pre-driven bike bought from a graduating senior, its twisted rear wheel brushing the fender with each revolution. Most off-campus sign-outs wanted to smoke or drink down here, but I was too scared of discovery and expulsion, content to wander as if lost, if only for an hour or two, until curfew called us back.*

Returning from the valley, we passed the red clay tennis courts beside Smith House, their nets still in place. *After dinner, in the fall and spring, during that golden half-hour between being excused from the dining room until organized study hall (in our dorm rooms or library, depending on behavioral and academic standing), occasionally I'd hit the ball with Lamb or others.*

On the courts' far side, hockey players laid out and erected the wood and wire "boards" for the natural-ice rink. Before we had ice, Coach Smith, a non-skater, had us shooting off plywood boards at goalies in pads and sneakers. When snowfall laid a solid base, we signed up for one-hour shifts, hosing it down throughout the night, when finished trudging with frozen gloves and glazed boots to Smith House where hot chocolate and cookies waited.

Speaking of Smith House, my sophomore year dorm, its homey, inviting, rooms were a delight after Rumsey. Mrs. Smith's ebullient smile, infectious laugh, and engaging personality occasionally invited us down to her and Mr. Smith's living room after study hall for tea or soda, and some sugary treat.

Late one winter night that year, my roommate woke me returning from his rendezvous with another drinker somewhere in Cornwall's moon shadows. He made it far enough into the room to just miss the end of my bed when throwing up jug wine all over the wall. Whether he didn't want to expose his sin to senior proctors by going to a toilet or couldn't make it there I never found out.

This same roommate invited a few of us to spend a Holden Caulfield weekend in New York City at his parent-less apartment. After a raucous train ride, laughter partnered with Rum Soaked Crooks, at Grand Central we stopped by the Oyster Bar to brandish our fake eighteen-year-old I.D.s. Almost fifteen years younger than Nick Carroway, I got drunk for the first time that night, and ever since have not been able to stomach screwdrivers.

Once past Smith House, the town tour completed, we left Cornwall Village for what, for me, will be the last time. Crossing Route 4, we headed toward West Cornwall on a scenic two-lane with hills, curves, and majestic trees shading our way. *Five miles distant, too far for us students to walk, my friends and I rode bikes, panting uphill, whizzing down.*

West Cornwall held a dragon's treasure back then, the mountain of gold including candy, chips, dips, and drinks from lemonade bottles to chocolate milk cartons, all un-available at the one retail outlet near school, the gas station (Sinclair?—I tend to remember a dinosaur on an unlit sign) behind Rumsey, down the hill, past the varsity field. The bagged loot brought back we stored in our rooms; although needing to last until the next trip, a week or more, with our ravenous, gluttonous dorm mates who didn't make the trip cajoling, bullying, and/or paying for our caches, its life span no more than a few days. Dairy and other products needing refrigeration we propped on winter windowsills, often confiscated by seniors, discovered and destroyed (or consumed?) by proctors, stolen by recalcitrant students, or

simply lost to wind or careless handling, dropping, explod-
ing one or two stories below.

Today the tiny town seemed even smaller than when explored as starving adolescents. We crossed the Housatonic on the famous covered bridge and drove that scenic river road toward Marvelwood's new Skiff Mountain campus. When Siri led us up a steep, dark, narrow, winding gravel road, we doubted her expertise and began to believe ourselves lost. Suddenly we mounted a summit, the sky opened, and the new school blossomed around us, the green background lush and inviting, the buildings modern and angular. All three of us laughed, thinking nowhere else in Connecticut could a campus be more sequestered from the world than in Cornwall Village. But, perhaps, this was.

Bob Bodkin's vision may have been hampered by the small town's insularity and housing choices. *When seated for morning assembly in metal folding chairs or in hardback wooden chairs at dining room tables, perhaps what I felt back then, if it could have been verbalized, was a lack of coherence, of fitting in, this desolate beauty so radically different from Chicago's Gold Coast that my four years of boarding school seemed an out-of-body experience. A ghosting.*

One final anecdote. When dining room seating assignments were posted every week, groans erupted from those sentenced to the headmaster's table. Not only were exquisite table manners expected with the likes of Mr. and Mrs. Bodkin present, but with family style serving, portions were handed out slowly, deliberately, preventing the table's waiter (underclassmen took turns) from going back to the kitchen for seconds (when available) before other tables with less scrupulous manners.

At lunch one day, sitting stiffly and quietly, keeping my elbows off the table and trying not to attract attention, Mrs. Bodkin, model of propriety and conversational acumen, pose a question to the assembled sufferers, fake smiles glued on: "Do you believe in capital punishment?"

A couple of students, probably upperclassmen, mumbled something abstract and non-committal, their answers lost to me now. When no one else spoke, the headmaster's wife turned to me. "What about you?"

Having no clue what "capital punishment" meant other than it might have something to do with the alphabet taking note of proper nouns, I wavered, dodged, hummed, and hawed until she took mercy on my obvious ignorance and embarrassment and picked her next victim.

Let that moment serve as a metonymy for my years at Marvelwood (1963-7). I wasn't ready for it, but I was better off for it. Blindsided by the loneliness of a long-distant student, I nevertheless left four years later knowing more about myself than the academic curricula. The greatest gift the school offered, Edwin Sundt, my freshman and junior year English teacher, encouraged my writing, especially by selecting me as co-editor of Marvelit, *the Marvelwood literary magazine.* I still have faded carbon copies of my feeble attempts at fiction and poetry that slowly disappear, thankfully, with every passing year.

The John Updike write-for-a-living plan didn't pan out for me, but I published a couple of innovative short fiction chapbooks, a book of poetry, and a collection of my local newspaper columns in which I continually throw my wife and children under the bus. Even though written over the next half century, these books surely began in some fashion the day that school van, carrying a scared, homesick, lonely kid from Chicago first turned south off Route 4 and entered for the first time the village that would be his home for the next four years.

And, in many ways, his home for the next fifty-two.

Making Room

Jamie A. Hughes

In my imagination, Eden smells like wet paint. It was a place for such beauty-making and name-giving, every square inch an opportunity to leave a mark, a stroke, a flourish of yourself. But when the time came for Adam and Eve to go, before the cherub waggled his flaming sword at them and said to get lost, God took out a can or two, wiped the place clean, and prepared to start again.

If this thought seems odd to you, your parents probably still live in the house where you grew up. There are still marks on a doorway, likely the kitchen, charting your growth—a neat date and your initials by each line. But that's not the case for my family. We knew no such permanence, never had the time to amass a respectable amount of clutter to hold a garage sale. No, every two or so years, we'd move into a rented house in some new town, a virginal space seemingly without blemish. Sometimes, I imagined we were explorers setting foot on alien soil, the first to breathe the air and settle the terrain. The first to say, *This is our home.* We were the only ones who ever hung family photographs on its walls, put dents in the chair rail when we stood up too quickly at the kitchen table, or spilled cleaning supplies under the sink.

We'd make a life for ourselves in each of these spaces; my parents, my brother, and I would find new friends. We'd host game nights and holiday get-togethers. We'd let junk mail pile up on the counter and dust congregate on window blinds. Over time, the place would slowly start to gather scents like Saturday-morning bacon and eggs, gym socks, and Estée Lauder's Beautiful, which my mother faithfully applied to her wrists and the graceful curve of her neck each workday. But eventually, we'd get the call telling us that Dad had been promoted and it was time to pack up and move on to the next undiscovered country.

We'd clean the carpets and scrub the grout, take down the photos and patch holes in the walls. Then we'd crack open a new can of eggshell white paint and erase ourselves. Every ding and scratch, any evidence we were ever there was removed in an afternoon. It was like we were covering our tracks; though I was never sure what we were running from (or to). And I never asked. I just locked the door, left the key under the doormat for the landlord, and disappeared into the back of a van.

At first, I enjoyed the going. Each new place was a fresh start, a chance to escape past mistakes and reinvent myself somewhere with no memory of me (or I of it). Like a chambered nautilus, I'd outgrow a space, seal it off, an emigrate to the next. But in time, our houses started to feel less like spaces to explore, places we were welcome to dwell in and fill, and more like stages decorated with a truck full of props we'd move from venue to venue as we performed our little melodrama in another rented space. *One night only! The Hill Family Shitshow! Not to be missed, ladies and gents!*

I was installed and erased so many times, the edges started to blur. Were the white spaces we walked into and left behind really blank canvases like I imagined, or was it all some kind of trick? I started to wonder if anything I did mattered, if anything I did would last, or if it all could simply be painted over and out of existence. I felt like the narrator of Charlotte Perkins Gilman's "The Yellow Wallpaper" in reverse, disappearing into the blankness rather than trying to claw my way out of a garish pattern.

As a result, I never acquired a knack for permanence. Maybe I could have, but I was never given a chance to "put the wagon wheels out in front of a ranch" as it were and bestow a folksy name on any given place. Truth be told, I've never felt sure enough of a space—or of myself in it— to know for sure if I *could* stay put. And I fear I've missed my chance to understand rootedness after all these years; it's a like a foreign language I can never learn to speak.

My rebellion began sometime in the early 90s when I was in middle school. (Isn't that when *all* good insubordinate streaks begin?) Rather than paint over every defect and make the walls blank as a new hard drive, I'd leave a single pin hole—usually from one of the corners of my much loved and very dog-eared posters. And as I rolled them up and put them back in a tube, I imagined Kurt Cobain, Layne Staley, and Zack de la Rocha were winking at me, pleased with my efforts at anti-authoritarianism.

"Leave it better than you found it," my dad would always say as we hustled around picking up trash and staging things for the movers. But as I spackled and painted (a job inherited from him because I was patient and attentive to detail) I looked for the perfect hole to leave behind—usually one at eye level that couldn't be missed by someone who was *not* in a hurry. And without a word to anyone, I'd lift my brush slightly from the wall mid-stroke. Like the angel of death, I'd pass over the hole and let it be. And if there wasn't a good one to be had, I *made* it.

It was an act of defiance, a refusal to vanish as if I never was. That tiny hole was a way for me to tell someone, *anyone*, that she was not alone, that someone had been there before her, someone who had packed up and moved on, hopefully to better things and broader horizons. For a decade plus, I was like Georges Seurat, creating a pointillism masterwork—my canvas three states wide—one tiny dot at a time. Sometimes though, I wish I could have left a pushpin behind, something to wrap a piece of red thread around. Maybe then, like Theseus, I could have retraced the steps through my own labyrinth of identical houses, found a way back to myself rather than spend all those prime early-adulthood years lost and bewildered, pieces of me left in cardboard boxes made floppy with constant refolding.

The Japanese, as they are wont to do, have a word for what I was trying to craft: *Ma*. A combination of the characters for *door* and *moon*, this word visually depicts a delicate moment of shimmering light seeping through the chink in an entryway. *Ma* is the space between two things or events, intangible and entirely necessary. A word without Western equivalent. It is the reason the Japanese pause at the end of their bows and practice the art of *Ikebana* (flower arranging) with a skill no other culture on Earth can match.

The word *Ma* roughly translates as "gap," "pause," or

"space between two structural parts," and it spans both space and time. It is not something can be measured or quantified, only experienced. There needs to be enough margin—enough *Ma*—around objects and actions to give them wholeness. And it is in those little voids (after all, not every void implies a lack) that we find balance and possibility. It's the reason why poets consider the absence of sound as well as words and why actors employ the pregnant pause. Because of *Ma*, there's as much beauty to be had in the silence between notes as there is in the melody a composer midwifes into the world.

In some way, that's what I was doing with a pushpin, the pointed end of a spackle tool, or if all else failed, the thumbnail of my right hand. Marking time. Balancing the scales. Making room. Defining myself in a world that would have otherwise have happily forgotten me.

The Neighborhood

Robert Iulo

Late on a July afternoon, when I worked for the Department of Buildings, I got a call from the Office of Emergency Management. They informed me that a four-story residence south of Houston Street on Mott was in imminent danger of collapse. This type of structural emergency wasn't anything I hadn't managed dozens of times since working for the Buildings Department, but this one would be personal. The "residence" was on the block where I grew up and just a few doors down from where I had lived. My job took me to what used to be simply "the neighborhood" and was now fashionable Nolita.

I contacted Tim, the Department duty engineer, and we arranged to meet at the site. As I drove up, the first thing I noticed was the shops at the street level of my childhood apartment building. They were different now. I recalled them starting with Sparney's Corner, a top-notch luncheonette where they made something called the Walk-a-Way Sundae - a small ice cream concoction in a cone-shaped paper go-cup. Buy it, and eat it walking away down the street. Then came a florist where I'd get my mother flowers on her birthday. Ballato's, an Italian restaurant well known to celebrities of the time, came next and was still there. As kids, if someone famous was having dinner, we'd jump up and down in front of the window, trying to catch a peek. Mr. Ballato would come out to chase us away. None of us liked him, and we never ate there. Our mothers, proud Italian cooks, wouldn't stoop to eating in an Italian restaurant. The row of shops ended with Frank's Candy Store. Small but well-stocked, you could get anything there, from school supplies and newspapers to greeting cards and coffee. He made the best soda fountain drinks - cherry cokes, egg creams, and in summer, lime Rickeys.

I parked and met Tim. We found the Fire Department had tied off the endangered area with caution tape. The occupants were on the opposite side of the street, waiting for news on the fate of their apartments and belongings. They were young professionals and nothing like the first and second-generation Italian neighbors I grew up with there. The Incident Commander briefed us. Rain had flooded an excavation, causing a slight shift in the adjacent building. Tim and I entered to do an assessment.

What used to be a butcher shop on the ground floor was now a Japanese restaurant with a sushi bar in the same place the butcher counter had been. The butchers were Larry and Joe. I'd pick up orders from them that my mother had called in. They would give me beef bones as a treat for my dog Duke, a boxer I often took with me. Over the years since I'd moved on, I went back to visit my parents but didn't spend any time on the street and keep up with how it had changed. After my parents died, I had no reason to go to Mott Street at all and didn't expect the transformation that had occurred.

We went to the roof to observe the excavation from above. I couldn't help looking into the backyards and Saint Patrick's Old Cathedral's graveyard. We would sneak in at night to play hide-and-seek and ring-a-livio. A graveyard may seem a strange place to play, but it was one of the few areas in the neighborhood with grass and trees, and besides, the century-old gravestones seem to have been asking to be used as hiding places. I was baptized in this church and made my first Communion there. Every Sunday, my elementary school class assembled in the churchyard on Mott Street before going into the nine o'clock mass with nuns giving us directions, using scarcely more than stern looks and raised eyebrows.

I was here to do a job but found myself distracted by memories. We'd worked this type of incident many times before, and I wondered what Tim thought of my inattentiveness. We were a few blocks from Chinatown, where a friendly waiter at the Golden Dragon had taught me to use chopsticks. Then there was the whole Lower East Side with its Eastern European culture and food. As a kid, I assumed lox, smoked sturgeon, and chubs were Italian delicacies. Yiddish and Italian accents sounded pretty much the same to me then. When I asked about it, my mother explained how the blue numbers tattooed on some shopkeeper's forearms were one of the reasons my father had fought in the war.

The building owner let us into each apartment, and we saw some cracked plaster but no signs of structural damage. I knew the people who lived there when I was growing up. The layouts were the same, but the décor had drastically changed. The homey and comfortable were replaced by the sleek and modern. Looking out of a window down onto Mott Street, I thought, could this really have been where I learned to ride a two-wheeler and played kick-the-can and skelzy? Now I was back on that same street as a Buildings Department Assistant Commissioner inspecting a building I had walked past thousands of times as a child on my way to and from school.

We finished our inspection and concluded that the structure had shifted. Damage was minor, with no danger of collapse. I contacted the general contractor, telling him bracing had to be installed immediately to prevent further movement. This work could be done within hours, and Tim would stay until completion. All that remained for me was to explain the situation to the tenants. They were standing in front of a stark, brightly lit storefront. In its window were a few pricey dresses and scarves hanging at odd angles. This used to be a loading dock with a granite base we used for playing stoop ball. Now it was a boutique. Even though we were standing on home base, I managed to block reminiscences of past stoop ball games and assure these people it would soon be safe for them to go back to their apartments. I wanted to say to them, "I used to live here. I played on this block." Instead, I told them what was being done to protect their homes.

As I walked to my car, I passed a store selling elegant Italian shoes in the same location where my aunt and uncle once had an Italian restaurant. They called it *Maria's*. There was no one in the family with that name. They just liked the sound of it. I thought of my uncle, who instead of preparing squid in the kitchen one sunny afternoon, opened the fire hydrant in front of the restaurant, set up a chair and started cleaning them there in a large pot. He was the color of an old penny, never missing an opportunity to sit in the sun and work on his tan. Distracted talking to a friend, he let the pot overflow, sending the squid floating away down the gutter. My friends and I were playing nearby, and he called us over to run down the block and get them. We made a game of it and managed to catch every squid. I'm sure anyone who witnessed this didn't order the calamari specials on the menu that night.

It was almost dark when I got back toward Houston Street where I'd parked. I looked at my old building and thought of my first friend, Johnny. We lived next door to each other and would play in the hallway outside our apartments. Being on the top floor, a skylight made our public playroom bright and cheerful. We laid out our toy soldiers on the floor tiles and steps leading to the roof, staging miniature battles. Our roof had clotheslines installed for the use of the tenants. I never hung any, but if there were an unexpected rainfall, I would help my mother take down her wash in a hurry. We all spent lots of time on the roof in summer; sunbathing, barbecuing, and gardening. That's where my uncle had his coop with over a hundred fancy pigeons. And quite a few of the tenants had flower boxes, so from May to September, our roof was as beautiful and fragrant as any backyard garden. Everyone knew everyone else who lived there, and we all kept our doors open. I'd say hello to a dozen neighbors and relatives as I ran up and down the stairs.

In the old days, at this time on a summer evening, clusters of women would be sitting on folding chairs arranged on the sidewalk in front of nearly every doorway. They'd gossip and talk about things important to them like the current prices of artichokes. I could almost see the ghosts of the usual group who would be around the entrance of my building, with my mother sitting there saying, "Don't come home too late."

I no longer knew anyone in the neighborhood where I had spent my childhood, and no one knew me. The people living there now were unaware of the comedies and tragedies once played out on those streets. That was all forgotten. Instead of dying, Mott Street had a new life, but the place I remembered was gone. It would have been sad to see boarded-up storefronts in vacant, graffiti-covered buildings, but this was a change and a feeling I hadn't expected. Everything was familiar to me, but still so different because although I wasn't a stranger to this place, I was to this time. It was a confusing mix of what I remembered and what was there now. The buildings and streets were the same, but what was going on in those buildings and on that street had no connection to my memories of what went on there before. It troubled me that the people living there now couldn't see what I saw. They couldn't see that where they were living wasn't just a quaint section of Manhattan with some historic buildings. It used to be a neighborhood with a heart and soul that made me what I would become. And no one knew it but me.

The House and Its Moments

Kyle Ingrid Johnson

The moment lasted fifteen years. Falling in love came first, followed by discovery of the various mutilations, hearing the macabre stories, and all the while working to restore the beauty within.

The house was nearly 130 years old when first we saw it, a group of friends who were thinking of buying it together. It had five floors and eighteen rooms, certainly space enough for all of us.

Each one noticed something different: the Corinthian columns and capitals, the statuary nooks, the beehive oven, the defunct servants' bell system, the old tin Coca-Cola signs nailed for fireproofing to the inside of the furnace room door, the tiny maid's room under the eaves, the front and back stair cases, the lions' faces adorning the front doors, the dentil work along the roofline, and the ivory marble fireplaces in the parlors with their carved, cascading cornucopias.

We also took note of the three mildewed bathrooms, each one worse than the last. One with a clawfoot tub, one with a rusted shower, and one with no usable parts at all. There were rooms with lowered, acoustic-tiled ceilings that stared down on us as suspiciously as we stared up at them. The double doors between the parlors were stuck on their tracks, and several panes of their exquisite etched glass were broken.

Eventually we came to THE ROOM. We all reacted differently. "Wow! What a lot of junk!" to "It smells like evil in here, doesn't it?" How could someone – anyone – store that much in one room? Granted, the room was large – about 20 ft x 15 ft – but the amount of storage placed on the floor seemed like room abuse. And it was. "Look," one of my friends pointed out. "The floor is sagging here ...and over there...oh, and here, too. It's actually caving in from the weight of all that stuff."

We wondered if there were any treasures, but it was unsafe to walk into the rubble; it was so obvious the floor was giving in. My eyes scanned the room for antique furniture, but what I saw was mostly debris. An ancient mattress leaned forward, falling slowly toward the hallway entrance where we were standing. "It's talking to us," someone said. "Creepy." I touched it and it shredded with hardly a whimper. It was stuffed with horsehair. "Wow! This is one old baby! This has seen some times!" I giggled, and another friend said, "Imagine if we could interview this mattress." Laughter. Silence. We looked at the pathetic object and its horsehair interior, but we all thought "Yeah. What if? What if we *could* interview the mattress? What would it tell us?"

The bigger question was: could we buy the house? Interest rates that year were 14%. After multiple tours, only two of us – my partner and myself - remained interested and determined, but we had the commitment of an artist we trusted. He didn't have cash to invest, but he was willing to rent from us in order to have a place to live and paint. By that time, I *had to buy the house*. It was talking to me. I admired it as I might physically admire a fantasy lover, and all its faults and broken parts hurt me and gnawed at me as I thought of ways to cheaply but effectively remedy them.

The house was located in an inner-city neighborhood that was racially and economically mixed. "You're moving *there*?" some people asked. But *there* felt comfortable to us. On both sides were buildings almost identical to ours that had once been elegant single-family homes. Now a rooming house sat on one side of us, and the other held an African-American family from the South; their patriarch had bought it on the G.I. bill after WWII. They also rent-ed rooms. Our neighbors liked us. We fit in. We were an eclectic group: black, white, gay, straight. We were kind of like everyone else on the street. The only thing that seemed to make us different is that we were in love with our house and the beauty of it. No one else seemed to no-tice their architectural surroundings, only paying attention to the people that inhabited them.

Once moved into the house – my partner with me and our artist friend upstairs - we kept discovering what was missing. In the front hallway, the doors were framed with Corinthian columns and crowned by Corinthian capitals. I had somehow, on my many tours of the building before purchase, had my mind tricked into believing that the triple parlors had doors and windows with the same Corinthian patterns. It wasn't until I was standing on a ladder with a can of paint that I realized that someone, at some point in time, had actually cut out every Corinthian capital through-out those rooms. I was horrified. Sad. I missed something I had never had. Why had someone done that? Did they think the capitals were ugly and removed them to make the rooms look more modern? Did they need cash and cut them out to sell to an antique dealer or a preservation carpenter? It seemed like such a simple thing, but it bothered me for years. Someone had mutilated our house. Someone had snatched away an integral part of its beauty, leaving it still glorious, but lacking something, almost like a missing tooth in an otherwise healthy mouth.

"Mamacita! Mira! Mira! We have them here. I can let you in some night and you can carve them all out and we will take away those boards in your parlor and replace them with these. They are the same, I swear. *Mira!"* One of our more charming neighbors, a Puerto Rican drag queen (who nowadays might be considered a Latinx transgendered person) learned of my despair over the missing Corinthian capitals. It was true that the architecture in the rooming house was identical. Undoubtedly the same craftsmen had worked on both buildings. The capitals would fit perfectly. *"C'mon! Vamos! Mamacita, it is the answer to your prayers."* It was, in a way, and I knew the owner of the rooming house wouldn't know a Corinthian capital from a crown on a Queen, lived in another state and cared only about the rents. I could probably get away with it, but I couldn't do it. To destroy beauty in order to replace it elsewhere seemed like an odd concept.

In *Uncontrollable Beauty,* a book of essays edited by Bill Beckley and David Shapiro, writer John Hejduk writes "Sentences on the House and Other Sentences," an essay in list form in which he explores beauty within a house, the soul of a house, and later – at the end – how the house speaks about and relates to death. Hejduk writes: *"The house searches for its lost occupants."* We, too, searched for the lost occupants of the house. I went to the Boston Public Library and scrolled through rolls of microfilm and leafed through copies of old City Directories.

Eventually I had pages of information: who had built the house and when, how it had first been sold and to whom, records of owners selling and owners buying. I learned that it sold for $11,000 when new in 1855, and then sold for increasingly lower and lower prices through the years, even as low as $4,000 in 1944 before finally seeing the prices start to go up again in 1975.

All that information was interesting, but it didn't really tell me who had *lived* in the house, only who had owned it. I knew from tracing my fingers over the numbers on various rooms in my home that it had once been used as a rooming house. Roomers are not exactly the kind who get their names in standard municipal records. Their lives go unrecorded. A house might be stunning, but its inhabitants are just regular people who come and go.

The elders of the street, mostly women, told me stories. "That was one bad rooming house back in the day. All sorts of things happened there. Fights, stabbings, and I think I remember something about a gun. But then Miss Hester bought the place, and she ran a respectable rooming house with nice people."

The three of us who lived there felt perfectly comfortable in the house. We resided there compatibly, our creativity aided by the house or, at least, the house didn't hinder it. All three of us pursued some form of self-expression in our work: painting, writing, photography, and the house didn't seem to mind. But occasionally it spoke up as if it wanted us to pay attention to something. The ground-floor hallway often felt as though one were walking through walls of cobwebs, yet no cobwebs were visible. Often, the doorbell rang, but no one was there. The door of my writing room had a doorknob that occasionally turned and turned as if someone were trying to get in from the hallway. Our artist friend was planting flowers in the front garden one day and dug up a voodoo doll stuffed into a small glass jar filled with a kind of iridescent lilac-colored powder. We didn't open it for fear of what the powder might contain. Inside, we could see a tiny slip of paper with a name written on it. We tamped down our curiosity and still refused to open the jar in order to read the name, but we kept the odd bottle on a shelf for years, a conversation piece for guests.

We had two separate psychics – neither one charged any money, interestingly enough - come in to "read" the house. One was such an obvious sham that we could hardly hold back our laughter. She had either researched or guessed correctly as to the date the house was built, and her entire reading consisted of spotting people in fashions from the period. Around each corner she would exclaim: "And here I see a man in uniform from the Civil War; he is on the Union side." She went into great raptures as she "encountered" women dressed over layers of petticoats, crinolines, and hoop skirts. She was a whirlwind of fashion hallucination as she made her way through each floor of the house, never mentioning feelings, hints of past events, or messages from the beyond. Not that we were really expecting her to; we were going through the entire experience to see what might happen, not because we really believed in psychics. We were finished with her, though, by the time we reached the ground-floor rear and THE room, the room of the horsehair mattress. "Oh! I see ...can you see her? A very pale woman; she might be Irish. She is over in the corner by the beehive oven, and she is dressed in a maid's uniform." Well, of course.

The other psychic, though, seemed to hit on *something*. There were places in the house where residents and guests pointed out strange feelings, and – although we did not mention this to the psychic beforehand – these were the areas he gravitated to. "Someone was pushed down the stairs here," he said very matter-of-factly as he stood on the fifth floor outside the little room that had housed a servant a century ago. "It was a hard push. I am not quite sure if someone died, but I feel a lot of pain." Later, he was in the room on the ground floor that had once housed years of debris alongside the infamous horsehair mattress. "Oh! This is the worst room in the house. Someone was shot here."

We didn't use that room much even though it held the massive beehive oven and the intriguing, nonworking servants' call bell. We had a washer and dryer installed, and the room was used for laundry and storage. It was true that we didn't linger there. Even the cats avoided that room.

"Moldings hide the wounds of a house." That is what Hejduk tells us in his essay. The triple parlors held fascinating moldings; I know because I painted every inch of them in all three rooms. They were handcrafted by impressive tradesmen who made those sorts of decorative items every day of their working lives. They didn't know that well over a century later, their workmanship would be admired so keenly. Reading Hejduk reminded me of painting those moldings with their winding leaf pattern. What wounds were they hiding? I think it was the wounds that came after them, the cries and fears and complicated lives of the poor

who lived in the house when it held roomers. The beautiful house sheltered the fractured people with little money and hard lives.

So the house was built for glory and sold for high money, and for over sixty years, I discovered, it was owned by the same man. But after he died, the house started to fall apart, not only physically but in taking on the lives of its many and often violent inhabitants. Almost comically, Hejduk writes: *"Flowered wallpaper within a house makes the house feel an unease."* I had not yet read those lines when I painted over all the wallpaper. It was too much work to steam it off, and there was something disturbing about those cabbage roses – little faces with wicked eyes - staring at me each time I walked through the parlors.

The cycles: the wealthy came, the wealthy left, the poor came, and the poor stayed. When we arrived, the poor could be described as lower-middle-class. We, too, fell into that category. We didn't have very much money, but we had this big, once-grand house and a lot of energy and imagination.

After fifteen years, we sold the house. I knew it was going to tear me apart. I thought about the advantages of taking anti-depressants ahead of time in case leaving our castle left me bereft. I wrote about the house in my journals. It was like leaving a lover. The gorgeous elegance of all that space, the incredibly long history, the weird tales and even stranger "spots" that made one shiver. It was all glorious, and I was going to miss it. But the property taxes were rising quickly; they were up to one-third of my yearly take-home pay. And the house, despite all our cleaning and painting and repairing, was still old, still calling out for a complete renovation. The fire escape on the back brick wall had been cited as a hazard, and we couldn't even borrow enough money to replace or repair it.

And that leads to gentrification. The beauty and the bite of it. In most cities, and surely in Boston where we were, artists and gays have often been the ones to go into neighborhoods where others could never envision themselves, buy old buildings cheaply, and go on to lead creative lives. But as more and more adventurous and educated people came into such neighborhoods, the number of rooming houses and cheap apartments disappeared and, along with them, many of the poorer residents who had been the heart of the neighborhood for years.

We felt a bit guilty in selling our house. The realtor was surprised when a bidding war occurred, but at least it allowed us to choose our buyer. We bypassed the developer, scratched off the list the obnoxious interior decorators with their impossible, pretentious plans, and settled with a middle-aged woman buyer, someone who had lived in the neighborhood for years. She went on to keep the house for even longer than we had.

Last year she sold it. I looked up the transaction in the City records. She got nearly four times what she paid us for it. Good for her. We couldn't have waited that long. At the time I said I had a big house and a small life, and I needed to trade that for a smaller house and a bigger life. And that happened.

A developer bought the house. Today there is a separate condominium on each of the five floors, and every one of them sold for well over a million dollars. The family from the South who lived next door sold two years after we did, and the rooming house followed. Today they are all superbly restored and, I am sure, very, very classy. The problem is, the community that was once there has disappeared. Who knows where all the poor and low-income people went? There are no rooming houses anymore. The City has a few licenses it gives out, but discourages them as it is thought that they bring down a neighborhood. I think the solution to the housing crisis is to go back to rooming houses. Boarding houses, even. A municipality consisting only of expensive condos and homeless shelters seems incongruous.

A few years after we sold, I ran into a former neighbor while downtown. She asked me where I was now living, and I asked her the same. "They ran me out," she said. "All these new people moved in. My landlord held off for a while, but he gave in and sold, too. I lost my cheap apartment. I'd been there forty years, you know? Well, let me tell you. Losing that apartment so some rich kids could move in was like a punch in the stomach." She made a fist and hit the air. "It hurt. It just about killed me."

And I wonder: did we play a part in this horror of gentrification? Did we buy a house because we fell in love with its beauty and, in selling it, help set off this violent wave of neighborhood change that forever uprooted the people who had been there longest?

Hejduk says: *"The house welcomes death after it has lived its life."* This is true. The building is no longer a house. It is a series of vertical condominiums. It has lost its soul.

My Brothers

Judy Johnson

There were always stories about my brothers, never facts. They were much older and left a trail of breadcrumbs behind. They had a band, which was escorted out of a town by the police for flirting too much with the local girls. They were beaten by the nuns with rulers, for what offenses we never heard. After summer camp they were forever banned from the Boy Scouts. Their names, Billy and Jody, were circulated from headmaster to headmaster; do not allow these boys to join your troop, "Danger, danger". All that was known was that it involved a sleeping bag and a small amount of smoke, or so they say. All story, never facts.

The stories began in Hibbing, where they were born. Their romanticized childhood played out in the back alley, between the long rows of tiny post war houses. In the dirt and red grit of the Iron Range, they played football and baseball. The rumor was that one of the boys in the gang was Bobby Zimmerman, who grew up to be Bob Dylan. In the morning Bobby, Billy and Jody would leave their houses, moms and chores behind, join the other boys behind the tomato plants and hollyhocks, and create the great Western adventure. They crushed the chamomile under their Roy Roger boots; raised dust with their stick ponies, brooms stolen from the kitchens. They cut stems from the willow trees and stripped the leaves; created whips for all sorts of devilish play. Their imaginations were birthed in those long summer afternoons with no TV and unsupervised backyards. When they were thirsty, they drank from a hose. Hunger drove them to the neighbor's raspberry patch. But the play never stopped until the mothers called at dinner time. And the gang of boys would depart to their various linoleum kitchens and waiting beef stew.

All these facts were pieced together, picked up one crumb at a time, over Thanksgiving turkeys and slide shows in the living room. Little Bobby Zimmerman, as my mother called him, came up often, our loose connection to fame. But the boys never talked about Bob, or their stick ponies. The cowboy games were replaced by 45's on the phonograph and hidden playboy magazines under the bed; the stuff of legends changed with time.

While in high school, the boys were rarely above ground. Their rooms were in the basement; a rank yellow tiled bathroom with shower, a wood paneled bedroom with two matching red plaid beds, and the darkroom with the poster of a naked girl way in the back. The hallway between these rooms had an 8'piece of ceiling panel, nailed to the wall, complete with asbestos. The boys used it as a dart board, with the large outline of a woman's body as the target. Certain body parts were worn down to the wood underneath from repeated strikes. Billy and John (he insisted on "John" once he turned 15) would come running in from school, stripping their ties and grey sweaters in the front hall as they grabbed a snack and headed downstairs. The sounds of Aretha Franklin and the Moody Blues pulsed under the floor between us and them. Girls would visit and disappear downstairs when Mom wasn't home. Their high-pitched laughter and perfume rose up from the dark landing. Bob Dylan was on the radio. *Lay, lady lay* came softly up the steps, the forbidden zone, the space between our world and theirs.

"Leave the boys alone," Mom always said. "They are too old for you."

Their friends were dark and smelly. They came and went, some to Vietnam, some to jail. The war played out in our basement, as did demonstrations and politics. Billy and John missed the draft. John had a water-skiing accident, sliced off part of his face leaving one eye hanging. The reconstruction kept him home when his number came up. Billy's number was never called, so they were a haven, solid ground for all the broken friends that returned. Mom said it was a miracle. But the miracles didn't always happen, and some were too fragile even in my brothers' safe haven. The blue smoke and sips from Father's whiskey supply did not keep their friends from crying.

> Mama, put my guns in the ground
> I can't shoot them anymore.
> That long black cloud is comin' down
> I feel I'm knockin' on heaven's door.

My brothers disappeared abruptly. John went off to college in Chicago, the great place of hot summers and the race riots. Every news report was followed by my mother's Hail Mary for his safety. He dated a girl from the south side, she was Polish and shy. He had friends that were black. He introduced us to men in bright clothing, who later died before anyone knew what aids meant. A new string of humanity stayed in his small dorm room as described in his letters. We visited him at the height of the riots; my mother concerned for his life and wanted to convince him to come home. Mom gave us instructions in the car as we pulled up to the dorm.

"Now, when I open this door you run as fast as you can to that building. That's your brother's dorm. Get inside quick. Don't look back, no matter what happens." She watched too much TV.

John didn't return to our house but brought his young wife and daughter to Minneapolis. He became a doting father and husband, living in uptown before it was cleaned up. The apartment was on the second floor of an old house, with caramel colored woodwork and windows that had to be pried open with a butter knife. They grew holly hocks in the back yard and had an ally where homeless men wandered at night. Anti-war posters were replaced with finger paintings, shot glasses with sippy cups. John went to work in a suit, the only executive with long hair and lamb chop sideburns. *Mr. Bo Jangles, dance* played on his car radio.

Billy joined the Christian Brothers, disappeared into a place that had a cinder block visiting room, painted white with a large wooden cross hanging on the wall. We wore Sunday dresses and our patent leather shoes to see him. He changed his name too, to Loren. I think it took 5 years before mother remembered to call him by that name. He sent pictures of the little rooms where the priests practiced saying mass to themselves. One was a picture of him in the long dark robe with the white square at the neck. Mother put it on the fridge; more images and breadcrumbs for us at home.

As he neared graduation, something fell apart. Loren no longer wanted to be a priest; neither did several of his friends. They all quit, telling the shocked and grieving parents by phone. They moved to an ancient barn up on the bluffs, drank wine and wrote poetry. They grew vegetables and wore sweaters with holes in the elbows. We visited once; to attend an Earth blessing ceremony. His roommate said the place was haunted, but with friendly spirits. Loren married a tall woman who took photos, covered the holes in the walls in black and white images, a coffee stain on the table, a blurry face covered in smoke. We brought Loren a winter coat because they only had a wood stove for heat. We left him there, on the bluff, with the wind blowing his long hair and my mother crying in the car.

> How does it feel
> To be on your own
> With no direction home
> Like a complete unknown
> Like a rolling stone?

Bobby Zimmerman was booed off the stage at the Hibbing High school when he played for a dance. His voice echoed off the marble columns, which the principal said was an insult to music. He left for new places, new faces. He changed his name and wrote songs, sang in his odd voice, and became world famous. Hibbing named a street after him and made the tiny post war house with the ally a site on the town tour. Dylan never returned to Hibbing.

My brothers never tried to reach him. But his music followed them. A family friend went to see Dylan in concert once. She dropped Billy and Jody's names to the security guard. After a few moments he escorted her backstage, to meet Bob, who asked about them. Said to say hi; breadcrumb confirmed.

We watched them scatter, further and further away. In the basement, behind the particle board doors and Jackson Pollock prints, my brothers' rooms were deserted. The plaid cotton bedspreads were dusty; the matching curtains drawn. Webs formed between the curtains and the glass; spider shadows scurried to the corners when we turned on the overhead light. The plastic model of a frog stared at the wall, the colored innards neatly displayed through the clear stiff skin, left over from science class years before. Tape scars remained on the dark paneling; Jimi Hendrix and the Rolling Stones, torn and faded. My sister and I found a box of 45's under the bed. Like an archaeologist, unearthing the long forgotten bits of other lives, a moment was captured, witnessed by another. A string of songs, sung by a childhood friend, traced all their lives. Loren and John were grown and gone before I even knew they were there. Now we had the scraps, as old and cracked as the Life Buoy soap left in their bathroom shower and Bob Dylan still playing on the radio.

Marking Our Place

Deb Liggett

Four miles into a fifty-mile Grand Canyon hike, I put down my pack, turned around and started walking backwards down the trail. Darkness was only an hour away. I heard Jay's footsteps stop, heard the extended pause and then he ever-so-patiently asked, "What are you doing?"

Jay and I have hiked together for forty years. Marriage came shortly after the hiking began and both the marriage and the hiking have endured. He always hikes behind and lets me set the pace. He has told me he wants to keep hiking this way for a long time to come, but at times like this he must wonder why.

There is no going back. Oh, sure we could climb back up to the rim, but then what? There was no water at the deserted trail head above, and it'd be a long wait until someone showed up.

The thigh muscles that controlled my knees went on strike. That wasn't the first time my knees rebelled, but it was the first time I had to drop my pack.

Jay shuttled his pack down a short distance, hiked back up to pick up my pack and carried it down ahead of us.

He repeated this routine six or seven times through the steepest descent. Meanwhile, I crept backwards down the trail. When the trail leveled out a bit, Jay moved the heavy things from my pack to his pack, and I shouldered my reduced load. I walked with the wobbly, uncertain gait of a stroke victim. Minutes before dark we reached a wide spot in the trail, set up our tarp and cooked noodles for dinner.

I was more shamefaced than alarmed. In case of a late start or recalcitrant knees, we carry extra water for contingencies. We had planned a leisurely hike. For the first time, we had the luxury of no jobs and no constraints except the return date on a backcountry permit. I slid into my sleeping bag, reasonably confident that my knees could be cajoled into working tomorrow and the day after that and the day after that. (The long haul up to the rim lay many days in the future.) As long as I kept eating, each day meant less weight in the pack.

We settled down for the night. As the sounds of our bedtime rustling eased, the wind dropped and I felt an ancient, infinite hush surround us. The Canyon was waiting for us.

Jay and I have completed our share of epic hikes, carrying dried salami, crackers and melting cheese. I have picked up and eaten Peanut M&Ms that I had dropped on a trail littered with mule dung. We have suffered dehydration and sunburn. We have returned to the Canyon again and again to renew our love affair.

Our route on this trip was down the South Bass Trail, across the Tonto Trail, and up and out the Hermit Trail to the South Rim. Most trails from the South Rim are steep and fall in a fairly direct route from rim to river. In contrast, the Tonto (Plateau) Trail is a level route in Grand Canyon terms, connecting side canyon to side canyon, traversing at an elevation halfway between rim and river. But the plateau (and hence the trail) is also synonymous with the most exposed, open, and unforgiving terrain in the Canyon. Unprepared hikers die on the Tonto. No shade and often no water, a lonely path wavering in the relentless heat. Even in the mild temperatures of late March, we respected the litany of deaths that marked this trail.

In 1857, Lt. Joseph Ives of the U.S. Army approached the rim, took one look at the canyon that blocked his way northward and passed summary judgment. "Ours has been the first, and will doubtless be the last party of whites to visit this profitless locality." It is impossible to imagine a better endorsement.

Come morning, my legs were rested from the unrelenting downhill of the previous day. We shifted some weight back to my pack. Stiffness dogged me for a few days, but the discomfort was the price of my walking meditation.

The trail has spacious views of the river and rim, and then cuts dramatically into the side canyons, seeking a way around them. In the places where the trail works its way around the drainages it is rough and notoriously difficult to follow. We measured our forward progress by the side canyons we navigated and collected their names like ribbons won at a fair.

Bass
Serpentine
Ruby
Topaz

Turquoise
Sapphire
Agate
Slate
Boucher
Travertine
Hermit

I concentrated on my feet and the ground while hiking, otherwise risking a face plant or a death-inviting somer-sault. The path revealed coyote scat containing a mouse jaw and part of bird skull; the new cones of the ancient Mormon tea; a small cylindrical cactus with long spines like a cat whisker; and a weathered puffball dried flat that looked like a sea star washed up on a desert shore.

Following the route takes some practice. To us, the trail takes on the persona of a living being, albeit one with a perverse sense of humor. This was a game of clues: a rock in the wrong place, a plant cocked at an odd angle, a single disembodied boot track, a half-standing cairn. There were times we could make out a remnant stretch of the trail miles ahead and times we couldn't solve the next ten feet. When the trail eluded me, Jay's extra height gave him an advan-tage. Sometimes the trail eased us into complacency, and sometimes we came to a standstill and milled around, con-fused. Behind us the last way mark might be visible but we moved forward, feeling our way, until we remembered to lift our heads to scan the horizon. We developed a rapport with the trail and could predict how it behaved in different situations. We made our way often with confidence, some-times with caution, skirting or conquering obstacles, but somehow always finding our footing and the path.

The routine was simple. Coffee. Oatmeal. Pack up camp. Drink water. Eat lunch. Fill water bottles. All the while we joked about the other person's trail farts (I don't have any) and whined good naturedly about the trail being too steep, too flat, someone didn't bring enough chocolate, someone put a rock under my sleeping pad, and a host of other invented complaints. We stopped for a water break in mid-afternoon and began our campsite search. Set up camp. Cup of tea. Dinner. Bed. Repeat. Somewhere we managed to find time to meander down the trail. It was in this reassuring and steady way that we marked the passing of our days and nights, our hikes, our marriage, our life.

We laughed when we spotted O'Ryan [sic], the famous "Irish" constellation, over the South Rim. First, I saw the middle star in his belt and then the Dog Star, Sirius, then Aldebaran and Betelgeuse. I identified Scorpio, the Big Dipper and the Pleiades. I recognize my old friends with the strange names, time and time again, even after periods of long absence. I greeted each star or constellation individually, out loud and by name, the dark sky a part of the tapestry that secures me to this familiar place.

It's a fact that when God made the universe She started with these very same stars. One day after work, God was tidying up the universe, washing the windows, vacuuming under the beds, and sweeping the dirt and dog hair from the kitchen floor. Almost as an afterthought, She created the planets. Unlike the other planets, the poor dust bunny that was Earth had no rings and only one paltry moon. But God gave this small planet something else—the divine spark of life. In this deep incision in the Earth's crust, those paying attention see the beginning of the universe in the night sky, and in the layers of rock beneath their feet can trace the evolution of life. A privileged view.

Midway through our trip, as we began our campsite search, seven desert bighorn sheep appeared. I deduced that it was a bachelor herd, the guys kicked out by the ewes while they calved. We found a flat rock for the kitchen, a space for the tarp, and a view of the river below. After sunset, a sliver of a moon hovered in the western sky and the quiet slipped in. We were almost asleep when we both sat up halfway and listened intently. We heard, perhaps not footsteps, but a hint of movement, outside the tarp. Simultaneously we whispered, "Sheep!" and then the explosion of twenty-eight hooves beat a swift retreat.

The next day in the soft sand under a rock overhang we found partially buried scat and tracks with no claw marks visible—classic cat sign. Cats can retract their claws, unlike coyotes, whose claw marks are clearly visible. The tracks were large and we knew there was a mountain lion in the neighborhood. Sheep beware.

On yet another morning when we exited the tarp, Jay and I each uncovered a 1982 penny in the dirt. It was a cosmic *woo woo* kind of moment. What were the chances of both of us finding a penny in the dirt in the middle of an untracked expanse of shale and prickly pear?

When we chose the campsite the night before, well off the trail and next to no particular monument or mark, there was no recent human sign. But we'd made the same choice as the 1982 Penny People. A good campsite to one generation makes a good campsite for the next generation; the holy qualities of a place to one people are felt by another people in another century.

Making our way east, we named our campsites: Bass

Trail, Pack Rat Rock, Bighorn, Two-Penny, Almost Agate, Red Dirt and Condor. At the Almost Agate camp I built small shrines, rock statuary. I built them to honor our joy in the moment and pay homage to the place. I know the shrines are impermanent and I intended them to be so, destroying them before we departed, leaving no sign of our presence. I was saddened, though, and wished that the building of stone shrines could freeze these perfect days in time, forever. I like to think that if I lost my way in the years ahead in the world above the rim that I could return and find these rocks standing, marking my place and my way.

We hiked. The sky was sunny. It was overcast. It was rainy, the weather mild between the raindrops. Hail fell one afternoon and we sought refuge under a rock overhang. The trail wandered perilously close to the steep drop-off to the river and I planted my feet with deliberation, buffeted by the wind.

We hiked. This was the put-one-foot-in-front-of-the-other part of the program. I availed myself of every opportunity to stop. One day I stopped mid-stride and broke into enthusiastic applause. Jay stopped and applauded, too. A century plant (agave) was sending forth a central stalk—thick as your arm and twice the height of a person—preparing to bloom. Popular belief says the plant blooms once every hundred years and then dies, a one-time spectacle worthy of our applause.

We hiked. We tried to go light. Even so, Jay said we have more things on our backpacking trips than some entire cultures have objects. He's right. Packs, sleeping bags and pads, tarp and stakes, ground cloth, gas canisters, stove, cook kit, scrubber, lighter, water bottles, iodine tablets, soap, toilet paper, walking sticks, medical kit, and maps made up our communal gear. Rain gear, coat, vest, winter hat, gloves, camp shoes, long underwear, extra socks and underwear, knee brace, small personal kits, paperback book, journal, pen and pencil. Not quite the bare essentials, but close to it. Finally, we carried our food and water, the clothing on our backs, and the boots on our feet. A simple, utilitarian and fulfilling life is possible.

Jay woke first in the mornings and lay in wait, trying to elicit nonsensical responses from me as I slowly came to life. He delights in tormenting me. One day, inspired by the tag on his sleeping bag, I woke to a poem recitation.

> Care Instructions:
> Add pretty girl
> to purple sleeping bag.
> Stir in love.
> Treat gently.

As the days passed, I became the garbage scow. This was a low-weight, high-volume kind of duty. In addition to the trash, I carried the extra toilet paper, the titanium cook kit, the freeze-dried food and the empty gas canister. I was more than an unwashed pretty face. I was useful.

It seemed so easy to clean up after ourselves, to be thoughtful about how much gear and fuel we planned to use. Before the trip we stripped the food of packaging material when we organized our meals. Our packs, empty or full, were tidy and ship-shape. We took pride in leaving no sign of our passing. As I hiked, I thought about what a better place the world could be with the simple ethic of picking up our own messes and tidying up after ourselves.

Humans are not well-adapted to the desert. We have no specialized kidneys, we can't obtain enough moisture from eating seeds, our ears aren't large enough to act as heat exchangers and our eyesight is poor and limits our activity in the cool hours of the night. The human adaptation to heat is to carry adequate water. But it is an adaptation with a weighty cost: eight pounds per gallon of water. One gallon of water per person per day in the desert. Minimum.

We inventory our odd assortment of full and empty water bottles, a bevy of one-liter containers. Some were clear, some collapsible, and at least one was stained a disgusting rust color from an overdose of purifying iodine. One quart was dosed with tropical punch Kool-Aid to hide an offending stain. Finally, a collapsible one-gallon blue nylon bag. These containers are the human invention, the adaptation that allows us to be nomads in this canyon.

On the trail, we met a pair of young women—schoolteachers, we discovered—hiking in the opposite direction. They inquired about our location and we confirmed what they had hoped—there was water in this drainage. They missed the last water because they didn't venture far enough off the trail to find a seep and were hiking with empty water bottles. One of them was sporting earbuds and listening to music as she hiked. I wondered: How could she hear the canyon wrens?

A lizard skittered across the trail. It stopped and did pushups on a rock in the sun, greeting the morning warmth. "Hello, lizard," I said, and peered intently for signs of fur.

When Jay and I worked at the Canyon, a hiker once came into the backcountry office, asking for a permit to collect "furry lizards." The ranger diplomatically assured him that by definition, lizards do not have fur, but the guy insisted he had seen what he had seen. Rather than deal with the request (and for his own amusement) the ranger sent him to get a collecting permit. Another employee questioned the hiker. The request was straightforward. "I have been hiking on the Hermit Trail. I saw a furry lizard. I want to collect one." Furthermore, he asserted that "the government was probably keeping this scientific oddity under wraps."

The second employee, baffled by the request but wanting to share the joke, passed the hiker up to his boss, who listened with great interest. Then, with the wisdom of Solomon, the manager directed that a collecting permit be issued for "a furry lizard from the Hermit Trail area" and stipulated that "upon collection, the lizard will be housed in the park museum." This attack of common sense did not threaten the park or question the sanity of the visitor, so each party was satisfied. I smile and always watch for lizards with fur.

For days I punctuated our hike with calls of "Caterpillar alert!" I stutter-stepped and sang out to give Jay time to avoid squishing the prolific dark caterpillars that crossed the trail. We continued to stop and salute the blooming century plants. We broke into applause and sometimes I sang "Happy Birthday Dear Agave." We scared up five mule deer that looked at us in disbelief before they bolted. I am certain we looked ridiculous.

We were ridiculous.

The lunatics were loose in the Canyon and they were joyful!

Thoughts of hot water, beer, ice cream, and clean underwear begin to intrude at the end of every hike. We planned an early start the next morning, up the earthquake-ravaged

Hermit Trail to our re-entry into the world above the rim. Once there, we planned to sip coffee at the Hermit Rest gift shop. I would sit in the Teddy Roosevelt chair (Teddy really sat there) in front of the cavernous fireplace and delay our departure. No one would sit next to me, stained as I was with sweat and Canyon dirt.

The scuffs on our boots, the abraded, discolored places on my pack, the deep gouge on the fuel canister substitute for our campaign ribbons, another adventure notched on our metaphorical hiking staff. We point to the emblems with pride. We re-emerge with stories to tell.

We have camped beside prickly pear, Mormon tea and buckbrush, on red dirt and on bright turquoise shale, in the midst of house-sized rocks, next to fossil worm casings, and the frozen ripples of a primal sea. We built shrines and named the stars. We marked out our place on the planet, set up our tarp, and we were home.

Going Home Again

Mel Livatino

Leaving home was an immensity. I've been trying all my life to express that, the bigness of that. The central experience of my life.
—V. S. Naipaul

So primary is homesickness as a motive for writing fiction, so powerful the yearning to memorialize what we've lived, inhabited, been hurt by and loved, that the impulse often goes unacknowledged.
—Joyce Carol Oates

The past isn't dead; it isn't even past.—William Faulkner

You can't go home again.—Thomas Wolfe

Each spring for more than twenty years, from 1988 through 2010, I took house walks organized by women's organizations in the toney suburbs of Chicago's North Shore. On these walks no woman ever appeared alone; they came in twos and threes, mostly, it seemed to me, to parade their clothes, their hair, their nails, and to inspect everything and everyone with their finely reticulated sense of status. I, on the other hand, was a man alone on these walks: no companion, no fancy clothes, no status to speak of. I went because I loved the way light splayed itself over elegant walls, floors, and furniture, and made these houses glow. I went because all my life I have been looking for home.

My lifelong search for home has also taken me on another kind of house walk. On this walk I am again alone. No one else can take these walks, for they are through the homes of my childhood and youth. I take these walks not on actual foot but only in memory.

I once read of a soldier imprisoned in a North Vietnamese prison camp for six years, much of the time in solitary or near-solitary confinement. When asked what sustained him though those years, he replied that each day he played a round of golf on his favorite course in his imagination. He imagined every swing, watched the flight of every ball, felt the sun and air on his skin, and kept score for each hole. When the war ended, he returned home and shot an 86 his first time out. Those hundreds of imaginary rounds not only sustained him through all his years of imprisonment; they also kept his golf game in marvelous shape.

I don't take my imaginary walks though the houses I once lived in nearly as often as the soldier who played imaginary golf, nor have my walks sustained my life, but they have kept me close to the boy I once was and to the family I came from. My walks also entwine me with what lies at the bottom of the sweetest word in the English language: *home.* I take my imaginary walks in order to go home again.

The earliest home I can remember was an apartment building on the northwest corner of Southport and Irving Park Rd. in a working-class neighborhood on the north side of Chicago only a mile from Lake Michigan. We lived there from 1942 to 1944, when I was two, three, and four. Because they have so little ego, children absorb the world without filters, so that in later life they remember it like poets and painters. Only torn bits and pieces survive into adulthood, but those scraps are imbued with feelings that last a lifetime. The stairwell outside our second-floor apartment was such a scrap. Its gray-glass double-hung window gave onto an interior airshaft. The light from that window had no visible source—only the brick walls of the airshaft were visible—but this haunting light has remained vivid in my imagination for more than seventy years.

One afternoon in that apartment I wore a little boy's navy sailor suit and blew a boatswain's whistle so shrilly my babysitting grandmother yanked it from my mouth and I never saw it again. In that same living room I often played with a large green metal car on the gray carpet. I can still feel the shape of my small hand on the top of that car. Twenty-five years later my first new car, a VW Beetle, was as close to that color as I could get.

The Penesnaks lived in the apartment above us. Helen was a lovely woman with gorgeous curvy legs and a voice full of laughter. Decades later I dated women with legs just like hers. Her husband, Clyde, came to own a golf driving range at Harlem and Irving Park a few years later. I can still see the overhead lights of that range and my father hitting golf balls into the night sky. And a few years after that the driving range became one of the first shopping malls in the Midwest, the Harlem-Irving Plaza. There I took my first non-newspaper job selling Hardy Shoes when the Plaza opened in 1956. I shoved shoes on customers' feet on the very land where a few years earlier my father had powered golf balls into a nighttime sky. Though I never saw the couple after I turned ten, I have often wished I had a picture of that young woman.

When I was four or five my parents moved two and a half blocks away, to 3943 Marshfield. Though I have not been in that apartment in sixty-five years, I could walk you through it blindfolded. A bay window jutted out from the living room. Nights when my father was at work my mother often sat on a radiator in that bay watching the street turn dark, smoking one cigarette after another. My sister and I sat nearby watching her cigarette smoke curl up to the ceiling. Thirty-five years later my mother would die of severe emphysema.

On the north wall of that room, above the sofa, a large round mirror reflected the entranceway. One day when I was five or six, my mother ducked out to the grocery store leaving me home alone. Panic soon overwhelmed me. I was facing the mirror pulling on the shoulder straps of my beige corduroy overalls to go out searching for her – when over my shoulder I saw her coming in the front door. The terror of that "abandonment" has roiled my stomach on every long trip alone the rest of my life.

Early on summer mornings my father's friends would pick him up for golf in that room. They would pile out of their car, troop through the entranceway and stand tall as gods above me in that room, their voices and bodies huge, their laughter loud. Then my father would pick up his clubs from the entrance hall, go with them out the door, pass under the bay window, and drive off into the sunlight. Thirty years ago I took up golf, in part because of the sunlight of those mornings and the godliness of those men.

That apartment was chock-full of things virtually no one under the age of sixty has seen. In the dining room an oil stove weighed the air of the whole apartment with a heavy oily odor. In the kitchen a real icebox was filled each week by a man lugging a huge block of ice by tongs over his shoulder. A pot-bellied stove squatted on another wall, its yellow fire gleaming through a small glass window. I sometimes spat on its flat top just to hear the spittle sizzle. But my favorite thing in that kitchen was a radio broadcasting the adventures of *Our Gal Sunday* ("Can a young girl from a small mining town in Colorado find happiness with rich Lord....") and the wisdom of *Ma Perkins*.

Beside the kitchen was my parents' bedroom, where I once witnessed my father suffer a horrible bout of flu. Off the dining room was the bedroom where my sister and I used to lie in the dark listening to our parents and friends talk through a crack in the door.

Out the kitchen door a wooden porch butted up against the alley. Over the railing I periodically watched in amazement as a wiry man sitting high atop a large horse-drawn cart came rolling through the alley crying out, "rags o lion." He was a fixture of the era, a junk man collecting rags and old iron.

On that same porch I once constructed an airplane out of scrap wood found in the alley. On those two boards nailed together in the shape of a cross I rode the heavens of my young imagination as richly as any child today shoots down enemies on video games.

Across the alley was a cinder lot just behind Uncle Louie's tavern. Nights my father and friends sang barbershop harmony in that tavern, songs he also crooned in our apartment, mostly the Mills Brothers: "Lazy River," "Daddy's Little Girl," "Someday," "I'll Get By," "Paper Doll," "You Always Hurt the One You Love" – songs that still have the power to lift my young father's face and voice before my eyes.

At the rear of Uncle Louie's was a dilapidated shack with missing boards that revealed a horizontal two-by-four four feet off the ground. On it a friend and I used to place empty bottles – wine, whiskey, beer, milk, whatever littered the empty lot – and take turns throwing stones at them from the alley. Gallon milk bottles sounded the sweetest when they broke: a deep hollow POK. No one ever stopped us. In families with little money, these bottles and stones were our most wonderful toys.

Above the Italian family who lived on the second floor was a dark, dusty attic jumbled with hundreds of stored objects, but only one claimed my attention: my grandfather's cash register. A few years earlier, at sixty-three, he had collapsed of a heart attack outside his barbershop one morning. I have no memory of seeing him alive, and this was the only object of his I ever laid hands on. My sister and I used to bang its keys and watch large white shields with thick black numbers jump up in the register's window. After I turned nine I never saw the register again.

By August 1949 my father had scrimped a down-payment on a house at 4111 McVickers, in the far west of the city. For $11,500 we now owned a house that had been cobbled together one step at a time for four decades. The outside was sheathed in boring brown asphalt siding pretending to be bricks. The five-foot high basement forced everyone walking through it to adopt a permanent stoop. The center of the dining room floor, just above the basement's support pillars, was three inches higher than the periphery of the room. The garage at back was ready to topple.

Upstairs Gladys and Joe Sorci lived in a four-room

rental apartment with their two young children. Gladys was a gorgeous woman who used to throw her week's bedding laundry over the railing rather than carry it down to the basement. This practice irked my mother, but I think it was her beauty and self-assurance that really enraged her. Joe was a vet who had lost a leg during the war. In visits to the apartment I sometimes saw his plastic leg leaning against a wall. A few years after we bought the house from them, he was arrested for selling horse meat to butcher shops and passing it off as beef. When the news hit the front page of the *Sun-Times*, they quietly moved out, and a soft-spoken Latvian couple displaced by the war – D.P.s, we called them – moved in.

My father never stopped working on this house. Gravity and age relentlessly pulled at everything. To avoid filing for a permit (which in Chicago always meant paying off an inspector), my father and uncle tore down the garage and built a new one in a single weekend – when no one from the city would be around to check. My father also built a rock garden in the back yard, rebuilt the front porch, and tiled the kitchen and bathroom, but the first thing he and my mother did in the sweltering heat of that first August was to steam layer after layer of old wallpaper off the walls of the living room and dining room. My father never stopped repairing that house. I held the flashlight while he raged at whatever he could not tighten, loosen, fit, or make work. I quaked at every rage, thinking it my fault. At thirteen I was forced to pitch in. All alone I scraped and painted the entire two-story rear porch – punishing labor that took most of that scorching summer.

For the first few winters a coal furnace heated the house, and my father rose early to shovel coal into it.

Once or twice a winter coal men lugged bags of coal over their shoulders to a metal door in the side of our house, their faces and clothes encased in coal, only the whites of their eyes shining from their shrouds. After a few years we switched to an oil furnace. In a small corner of the basement my father built a workroom and workbench. A few feet away my mother did laundry in a round tub with ringers at the top. In the dark of that basement we played hide-and-seek with only the furnace's pilot light to guide us.

The house had only two tiny ill-situated bedrooms. The one off the living room belonged to our parents, while my sister and I shared the bedroom off the kitchen. When my sister turned eleven, my parents surrendered their bedroom to her and slept on a sleeper-sofa in the living room – an enormous sacrifice they made without complaint for the next four years.

The kitchen was small, plain, and strange. The refrigerator was not in the kitchen but at the back of the pantry: a Servel powered not by electricity but by *gas*. The sink was held up at one corner by a porcelain pillar leftover from the house's origins at the beginning of the century. Near the back door was a mangle for ironing clothes. It looked like a porcelain baby's coffin sitting on a chrome stand. On this mangle sat a large portable Zenith radio. Through its gold plastic grill one morning in January 1956 I heard Elvis's voice for the first time in my life. I was wearing a pink shirt with a large roll collar, a black string tie, and black pegged pants with a blue suede belt and blue suede shoes the morning Elvis first wailed "Heartbreak Hotel" into my ears.

The best thing about the house was that Chuck Cerniglia lived next door. Two years older than I, he was also much richer and cooler. He wore Levis and I Sears Roebuck cut-rate jeans; he wore white bucks and I the cheapest shoes in the store; he wore a tan suede jacket and I a shapeless thing from half-price Robert Hall. He owned not one but two electronic football games, a complete football outfit with pads and helmet, a pellet gun, and a .410 shotgun. His knotty pine TV room and finished basement were the envy of the neighborhood. I could only long for these things. When he was eighteen his parents bought him a brand-new all-white '57 Chevy convertible with a 270 h.p. engine: 4-barrel carb, dual exhausts, and fender skirts. It was the coolest thing in the world, and all I could do was look on in awe.

From the time I was nine till I was thirteen Chuck was my best friend and mentor; for those four years I felt bless-ed beyond measure. But when we were fifteen and thir-teen, he discovered girls, cars, parties, and cool friends his own age at his expensive high school. We were never close again, merely waving faint hellos at a distance for the next four years. In memory I still stand on the sidewalk in front of his house looking in the basement windows at the boy-girl parties I ached to be a part of – and never was.

Just as I was in the home stretch of my junior year, about to turn seventeen, we moved four blocks away to a small boxy Georgian at the corner of Mobile and Berteau. Though I could not know it at the time, the rest of my life would be shaped in this house. It was here my father coerced me into working for six years in the same printing plant as he. It was here I finally faced him down after years in the printing plant and told him that I would be going to college. It was here I decided on English as my major. Here I decided to become a college teacher. Here I met the woman who would become my wife and with whom I would have the three sons who have been at the center of my life for more than forty years. Here I received the teaching assistantship that launched me on my career as a college teacher. Without my knowing it, this plain boxy house became the crucible in which my life was shaped.

The room to which I was and still am most attached was my small bedroom on the second floor. On sunny days two windows let in brilliant cheering light. Every spring an apple tree blossomed just outside the east window. Those pink and white blossoms pressing against the window on sunny May mornings and afternoons are among the most beautiful things I've ever seen. Inside the room the most treasured thing was a cheap brass-wire bookcase beside my bed, for it was on those thin wires that I began collecting the books that have stirred and shaped and blessed the rest of my life. Cheap paperbacks, but they set me on the course of my life as a reader, writer, and teacher, but most of all someone who for half a century has thrilled to the pleasure and meaning of the written word.

On the top shelf of wires I also placed a reel-to-reel Silvertone tape recorder on which I recorded songs tangled up with the first girl I ever dated seriously and to whom I lost my heart before I knew I had a heart to lose. Her name was Sharon Evans and she lived in a distant suburb to which I traveled every chance I got, until a year into our relationship when her mother decided I was not right for Sharon and banned me from the house. After that, I could only sneak visits to her for a few minutes once a week while she was working in a drug store. In the only photo I have of her – a tiny thing smaller than my thumb – she is leaning forward, laughing, a boy's arm around her shoulder. She cut the boy out of the picture before she gave it to me, but I have never looked at that picture without seeing his curled fingers around her right shoulder. The song I listened to over and over each night on that tape recorder was the Fleetwoods' "Mr. Blue." Fifty-six years later that song still brings back that bedroom, that brass-wire bookcase, that recorder, that girl, and that lonely time in my life.

In the summer of 1960 my pining ended when I met an enchanting girl named Mary Lee Chval. She was car hopping at a Dog 'n' Suds for the summer. It was halfway between her parents' summer home and the dusty-pink Masonite trailer my parents called a summer home. We dated half a dozen times before she returned to her sorority house on the Urbana campus of the University of Illinois. I didn't know I was in love with her until our last date that summer – dinner at a fancy steak house I could not afford, followed by a midnight dip in her lake. On the walk down to the lake I turned to look at her, and by the light of a full moon saw for the first time that she was not just a swell girl but that she was also radiantly beautiful. We walked into the lake up to our waists and stood facing each other holding hands. For a few minutes we made the kind of nervous small talk young people make when they don't yet know how to talk with each other. Then across the lake from a radio or phonograph came Percy Faith's "Theme from a Summer Place" traveling the same path as the moonlight on the water right up to our waists.

I was utterly in love. We exchanged a letter or two that September, and then late one afternoon when I arrived home from work, my mother put a small blue envelope scented with Chanel No. 5 into my hands. I took it up to my bedroom, sat on the edge of my bed, and opened it with the nervous care of an eye surgeon, the same care I gave to all her letters. She was inviting me to come down for homecoming. I can still see that blue letter in my hands lit by the brilliant late-afternoon light from the south window and smell the Chanel on its pages. I bought new clothes, scrubbed the printer's ink from my hands and nails, and drove down for homecoming.

At dusk on an October Friday I cruised into the fairy tale world of sororities and fraternities all decked out for homecoming. Slowly I rolled through wood smoke and enchantment. That weekend and the rest of our Jay Gatsby/Daisy Buchanan relationship are etched forever in my memory. The tape recorder on the brass-wire bookcase in my bedroom now repeatedly played "Theme from a Summer Place." Fifty-five years later I cannot hear that song without remembering that summer, that weekend, that girl, and that letter read by the late afternoon light from the south window of my bedroom.

Four years after I met Mary Lee, I met the woman who would become my wife. We too met in late summer and soon "Strangers in the Night" and "Summer Wind" were on the recorder. Two years after we met, we married in the summer of 1966. I dressed for the wedding in that bedroom. The night before our wedding was the last time I ever slept in that house.

The only other room in the house to which I have a special attachment is the kitchen. It was under a fluorescent light in that room in 1958 that my father informed me that my wish to go to college after high school would not come to pass, that I would instead be going to work in the same printing plant he worked in. And it was under the same light five years later that I told him I would no longer continue working in the printing plant, that I would, after all, be going to college. Under the light of that kitchen I made the most important decision of my life.

2

Thomas Wolfe tells us we can't go home again. Thirty-two years after I lived at Southport and Irving and twenty-seven years after we moved out of Marshfield, I began teaching a mile away at Truman College. Occasionally I drove past these former homes. Over the last forty years I have never passed them without slowing down, looking, and remembering.

Once I poked my head in the entrance hall of the Southport building and smelled the same stale odor I remembered from when we lived there. It was the odor of every low-rent apartment entrance hall I have ever been in. The tiny white tiles on the floor were dirty; the paint on the walls, tired and dull. I wanted to go into an apartment, but which one had been ours? And how would I gain entrance? Tell them I was the ghost of times past? Besides, I knew I'd be disappointed. It wouldn't be our apartment; it would be someone else's twenty times over – someone down on his or her luck, for the neighborhood had been seedy for many years. Old newspapers blew in the wind outside and the windows hadn't been washed in ages.

Several times I walked the streets around the Marshfield flat. At the other end of the block from our house still stood the beige-shingled protestant church with the same iron-pipe railings leading up the stairs. The houses in between were still the same, but now they were fancied up and strange to my adult eyes. I felt like I was walking through a dream and yet not a dream. Déjà vu and not déjà vu. Uncle Louie's had long ago become Biasetti's Restaurant. Two blocks west on Irving, Manz Corporation, the first printing plant my father worked in – not the one I worked in with him – had closed its doors decades earlier and was now a sparkling clean business without the smell of printer's ink. All the storefronts on Irving and Ashland had changed to something else. Gone was Knopf Bakery, where my mother had briefly worked. Gone the dark brooding drug store run by the parents of my childhood friends, the Klein Brothers. Gone the National Tea Store with its prominent green and gold sign. The only place on Irving that remained the same was the diner across the street from Uncle Louie's. It was still a genuine diner, one of only three or four in a city of nearly three million inhabitants. It alone remained exactly the same as sixty years earlier—the same gray counter top, the same greasy chrome stools and stainless-steel walls, even a tired-looking man in a white paper wedge cap behind the counter.

I wanted to knock on the door of my old house and say, "I used to live here. Would you mind if I walked through?" But who would let me in, and what would I find?

I not only walked the McVickers block several times over the decades, but seven years ago gained admittance to the house itself for the first time in more than half a century. It was up for sale and the listing agent, thinking I was a prospective buyer, took me through. The tired brown asphalt shingles had been replaced by dismal gray asphalt shingles. The front porch my father had reconstructed had now become part of the living room. The rare built-in oak hutch that took up most of a dining room wall was now a gaping recess with a sagging sofa sitting in it. I opened the closet door in my tiny bedroom to discover a narrow wall inside the closet had been knocked down, revealing a stairwell to the second floor that had been hidden all the years I lived in that room. The apartment on the second floor was entirely gone. Nothing but unpainted rafters and subflooring remained. No plumbing. No kitchen. No heat. Just a bare dark attic. In my father's basement workroom the workbench he built and covered with a zinc printing plate still stood there. I wanted to pull a corner of the plate loose from the bench and turn it over to see the images and figure out the job it had once printed. The roof beam of the garage that my father and uncle constructed in a weekend sagged a foot in the center, and when I pushed on one of the walls it moved. A fullback hitting any wall would have toppled the entire structure. The rock garden my father had built flagstone by flagstone was gone. The white wire fence across which Chuck and I planned our adventures and over which I used to watch his mother hanging laundry on sunny summer days had been re-placed by a low dull-gray cyclone fence. A Mexican family with shaky English now lived in the house where the rich-est family in the neighborhood had once lived. In front of what had been the Lohrmann's house two doors north, an old man from Poland shuffled back and forth. He was wary, spoke no English, and seemed to have nothing else to do with his time.

Some years earlier I had also gone through the last house I lived in as a boy and a young man, the house that had become the crucible of my being. On a whim one day passing through the neighborhood I knocked on the door at Berteau and Mobile. The woman who answered the door had recently lost her husband after a long illness and possibly for that reason understood my visit to the past. I was struck by how small and cracker-box everything felt. Her husband's crank-up hospital bed covered with white sheets was still sitting in the middle of the living room making the rest of the room feel not much bigger than a large closet. How did we live in such a tiny place? I wondered. The dining room and kitchen looked smaller and flimsier than I remembered. How could this kitchen in which my father had sealed my future for five years and in which I unlocked my future at the end of those years be so small and insubstantial? It seemed I could push the walls down with my bare hands. My bedroom had always been small, and I asked if the apple blossoms still pressed against the east window in May. No, the woman said, there were no more blooms. There wasn't even a tree anymore. She planned to sell soon and start a new life.

William Faulkner was right: the past isn't dead; it isn't even past. Thomas Wolfe was also right: you can't go home again. You can visit the physical place you once called home, but it is no longer yours. It belongs to someone else now, and in a little while it will belong yet again to someone else and in a little more time to someone else. The only home you can go back to is the one in your memory. Only there does a beautiful woman with shapely young legs and a voice full of laughter live upstairs. Only there does a mirror reflect a missing mother coming in the door. Only there is Elvis still wailing "Heartbreak Hotel" to a boy in a pink shirt and string tie. Only there do the Fleetwoods still sing "Mr. Blue" over and over night after night into a dark bedroom. Only there is a twenty-year-old boy still sitting on a bed reading a scented blue letter by the brilliant light from a south window late on an autumn afternoon. Only there is a young man putting on a morning coat in the blazing sunlight of his wedding day to begin the rest of his life.

Birdland

Geoff Martin

We moved to Birdland when I was four years old. My family had only jumped a few streets over in town, from one former cornfield to another. But in leaving the semi-detached house on Aspen for a larger side-split on Oriole, my younger brother and I had crossed over into a wider, more labyrinthine world. This was a part of town to get lost in, what with its long arching streets and spiraled crescents darting off from dogleg turns and sudden short roads cutting through to other curlicue streets. Anti-grid by design, the subdivision's developer, on a whim in the mid-70s, had named each street for a different bird.

In short order, I knew all the names: Grosbeak intersected with Oriole about ten houses down—its stop sign signaling the initial limit to my free-pedaled territory. A year later, I was allowed to venture as far as Cedar Waxwing in one direction and Nighthawk in the other. Up and down Barnswallow along the town's western edge, I rode the bench seat three times weekly on our way to church. I had a friend over on Killdeer, ate chocolate bars from the corner store on Flamingo, went to middle school on Mockingbird.

As for the actual birds around me though, I was remarkably indifferent. Sure, I knew a robin to see one in April, hopping about our spongy yard hunting for worms. And if pressed, I could identify an oriole or cardinal but only because of Major League Baseball. Same for a blue jay, the Blue Jays, the back-to-back champions of my Ontario childhood. But truthfully, for most of my life, I have had a disconcertingly poor eye and ear for birds. Those streets back home were just blacktops to bike and friends' houses to find—not the common English names for animate flesh.

So, I had no inclination to ornithology, few kids do. Yet that speaks more to my own indifference than a lack of curiosity. There's also the fact that the birds we did have were more a declared nuisance than objects of study or appreciation. In the early 1990s, the town even went to war against them after fielding too many complaints, ironically enough, about all the birds in Birdland.

The problem was the grackles, the thousands of them. One summer, they chose to roost in the tall tulip trees clustered in several conjoined backyards nearby. Each evening, the branches heaved with their squabbles and dripped with their droppings. Lab tests came back listing e-coli and salmonella along with bacterial and fungal exposure risks with Latin names ("histaplasmosis," "cryptococcosis") that sounded as horrifying as the pulmonary diseases they represented. Naturally, the birds had to go.

Saddled as we thought we were with early bedtimes, my brother and I found ourselves trying to sleep at the edge of sound cannon booms and odd squiggling noises that the birdman—pest control—let loose each evening.

It didn't seem to work, as I recall. And the next summer, when the grackles gathered a few streets over, the cannon blasts grew fainter beyond the backlit pull-blind on our shared bedroom window.

Such were the bombs of my youth.

This matter of background, the ground zero of childhood, reminds me of the writer Michael Martone's insistence on drawing attention to the "ground situation" of a story. "It implies," he states from the open fields of Indiana, "that there is more in the background than just scenery. That 'the setting' is really integrated into the situation of the characters, that the characters are part of the setting, not just placed before it." His point is that all writing covers some kind of ground, so it's worth paying attention to the soil of a given story.

Perhaps it's our mutual experience, mine and Michael Martone's, of growing up on relatively flat, glaciated ground, but I like his line of thought. I'm no painter, but when I write it's the landscape of home and its various vantage points that preoccupy. The ground situation is more interesting to me now in my nascent middle years than a story's forward action. Which is odd, given that I had always thought the ground of my youth to be rather banal. Certainly, the fields surrounding Birdland lacked any kind of monumental panorama—no ocean's edge, no ice capped mountain, no seeming mystic ancient ruins. Just long horizon lines punctuated by grain silos and postage stamp forests.

From an early age, I had been eager to move off and away, curious to see the wider world from different heights and angles. And yet Birdland remains something of a nest I keep returning to, tethered as I am by my relations and by a persistent, recurring need to understand where I am now. It's as if I go back in order to measure how far off from home I've wandered.

Or maybe this is simply a commonplace adult experience for many of us. We lose ourselves into our individual lives and atomized jobs and then realize, a decade or four later—in the silences of late evening or from the corner of a therapist's couch—that the one thing we can never quite shake is the topography of our youth.

At the house on Oriole, we were soon six. In large families with shared bedrooms, the bathroom becomes the one place of privacy and withdrawal. It was the only room we could lock. And it was there in the windowless basement bathroom that I recall finding an owl shaped into dark wood grain, locked behind vertical grooves of paneling. Once noticed, it proved impossible to ignore. The two orb eyes were translucent, bearing a milky varnish. Their knotted swirls looked like elongated galaxy rings. They seemed, in hindsight, to swallow time.

Sitting up on the toilet, elbows boning into skinny legs, chin cradled in upturned palms, I stared back in a kind of quiet hypnosis, ignoring the pounding of others at the door. I tried to match its unblinking, nictitating membrane by crossing my own eyes, creating the illusion of greater depth. The ceiling and floor would crack ajar and the striated lines of wood grain would pop forward. I knew nothing then of augury, the ancient talent for mapping out omens in the flight paths of birds or reading prophecies transcribed into their entrails (I would have been suspicious of such dark illusions anyhow), but I sensed, in this owl, the offerings of a sign.

I was taught that God could speak not just through scripture but through the Book of Creation, the wider natural world, and who but God made this owl? It seemed placed there, imprinted with such obvious intent. And yet the owl's meaning evaded me, which is the trouble with signs—they carry the trouble of interpretation.

And it wasn't just the single owl that gave me pause. I had learned about the Nazca Lines the year before, had read about Peruvian pilots newly airborne in the 1930s swinging back around, swearing that there were enormous patterns etched into the desert plateau: a perfectly geometric hummingbird, a great, wide-feathered condor. Could the cursive streets of Birdland, I wondered, be patterned into some kind of shape or symbol, some signification inaccessible to those of us stuck to ground?

In the last several years, the ground situation of our collective stories has become, unavoidably, about the atmosphere and the environmental surround. No longer just backdrop, the setting is foregrounding itself. The climate *is* the climactic action. Now, we truly do gather all the news we need from the weather report.

In this emergent story cycle, we find ourselves confronting anew both the limits and the power of human life on planet Earth. And the feeling—if it can be so pinned down —is one of great and general unease. Among us North Americans, the bottomless consumers of the world, there's a wringing of hands and pointing of fingers and plugging of ears.

The other day, I awoke to an essay shared on Twitter that stated, "The period of world history since the 1980s has been the most extractive in human history." From bed, I doom-scrolled by thumb through the argument, sensing our ongoing, present-tense culpability for this growing climate crisis. "56% of the atmospheric carbon since the dawn of the industrial revolution," noted the writer, Ajay Singh Chaudhary, "has been produced in these past four decades." I have been alive for all but three of those years, a too-young GenXer and too-old Millennial, born to parents nearly too young to be called baby boomers. Wedged into the comforts of the Canadian middle class, I have participated, by the centrifugal energy of my life in the terrible plundering of the carbon stores of prehistory.

The problem is a grave one, endemic to and accusatory of an entire way of life. It has us now leaning over our steering wheels, starring through bug-less windshields, searching the skies for answers. We're wondering about the birds and worried about the bees. North America's land bird populations, another news article tells me, have declined by more than three billion over the past forty years, with dozens of avian species having lost more than fifty per cent of their populations. Snowy owls, I read, are down by sixty-four per cent. And now that we're losing the birds, the impulse is on to spot those we can. Our canaries in the continental coal mine.

A few years ago, while living in Chicago, I made an effort to begin taking note of the ecology of my city neighborhood. The false binaries between city and country, between culture and nature, no longer hold. But old myths die hard. They take effort to unlearn. I decided to start with the birdsong filtering through my apartment window. I wanted to live up to the reputation of someone who grew up in Birdland.

A week after my resolution to start noticing, I heard an auspicious, assonant hooting from the spruce branches that scraped the redbrick exterior of our third-floor walk-up. I was sure it was an owl. I just didn't know what species.

Later, while catching a ride with a friend and avid birder, I crowed about the owl outside my window. When I imitated its cooing sound, he grinned.

"Wait a minute," he said, fishing his right hand back through the clutter of Coke Zero bottles behind his seat. He pulled up a double CD of birdsong and punched through the tracks until landing on a field recording of exactly the call by my window. It was a mourning dove. A telephone-wire turtle dove. It certainly makes a plaintive call, but from his car's speakers, it was far less enigmatic than I had first heard in my ear. The mourning dove sounds nothing like an owl, any owl.

My ears, in other words, wanted immediate rarity but they weren't yet attuned to even the most common. The singular needs to be earned. It needs to be sought out and then waited for. It's an egg that needs sitting on.

I've been thinking about all this lately—my childhood, the birds, our changing climate—because my partner and I are nesting for the first time in our lives. We're camped out in a rented house near the Connecticut River, and C. is five months pregnant. With the homeowners returning in a few months, we're making plans for yet another move, this next one coming just ahead of the baby. Our own nest keeps shifting, and it's cause for some nervousness.

A nest, according to Merriam-Webster, is a specially modified structure that serves as an abode of animals, especially in their immature stages. And that's just the trouble. Given our own peripatetic behavior, it's been hard to imagine inviting a child to share in our rootlessness. We're the ones still maturing.

Our living arrangements have been so different from those of our parents, both sets of whom still live in the houses they bought in the 1980s. Theirs has been a long-term sedentariness, a committed placed-ness that I respect, even envy. And many of our friends and siblings who are now parents are ensconced in mortgaged houses or condos of their own.

Meanwhile, we feel a bit caught out-of-doors, albeit in winds of our own choosing. For the past decade and a half, our year-to-year rental agreements have enabled us to fly the coop as needed, sign a new lease, site-unseen, in some new city, and then set about making a temporary life for ourselves there. San Pedro, Costa Rica to Daejeon, South Korea. A twelve-month stay in Hamilton, Ontario, followed by seven years in Chicago. Short-term stints in Providence and Western Massachusetts. And up next, a transcontinental move, whether temporary or permanent we do not yet know, to San Francisco. Throughout the changing seasons of our itinerant, adult lives, we've continued to migrate.

And this whole time the question of children, whether to have one or two or none, has followed us around, happily ignored until it wouldn't be. We considered adoption but while we wait in the lengthening queue for a more secure status in the U.S. or some sudden, sizable uptick in our savings, the route seemed precarious. We wondered, too, about the resource demands of adding another human being to the planet, along with the ethics and challenges of raising a child within manifest global climate change. But then, following after the surprise of a miscarriage and the frank desire to try again, we now have this immanent child, one whose tiny feet and bird-bone elbows are pressing already at the uterine wall.

This baby, if given the gift of long life, will be eighty-one years old in 2100. That strange proximity to the next century makes me better understand the sociologist Elise Boulding's idea of the "200-hundred-year present"—the way in which each new day's oldest elder and youngest child tether together two centuries of time. My one great grandparent to hold me in her arms was born exactly a century ago. And her elders, her own grandparents for example, were all born before 1850, at the dawn of the industrial revolution. This is how swiftly the centuries spill forward, seven generations to now. How long-reaching and consequential our actions. And our inactions.

Recently, the baby passed twenty-four weeks of development in utero, the threshold of viability our midwife pronounced with a smile, so this time we've begun to nest with decisiveness. But rather than scrubbing the baseboards, which the *Complete Pregnancy Encyclopedia* describes as "a well-documented phenomenon of nesting," our readying thus far looks more like a great off-loading.

At long last, I'm jettisoning my old notes from college. Thousands of blue-inked pages scrawled out in the early-aughts, foldered according to course title, and hauled up and down the stairs of a dozen-odd apartments and storage basements. I'm refusing to move them all again.

And yet I can't help but peruse the papers a final time, which is why the task is taking up entire evenings instead of providing immediate fuel for one great conflagration in the backyard. Midway through the Classics 101 folder, I stumbled across a half-remembered lecture on the symbolism of the owl. Athena's ancient emblem, the owl marked the goddess of wisdom and stood as guardian of the Acropolis. Its eyes, rounded spirals like knots of wood, were stamped on Greek coins to signify a vigilance over earthly commerce.

The notes reminded me of Kathryn Miles's essay "To Wit, To Woo," where she describes the owl as a species out-of-joint in a warming world, irrupting now in haunted daylight. For Miles, the barred owl perched in her sunlit backyard in Maine stares back impassively, full of complex, mythic associations: symbol of Greek wisdom and justice, yes, but also the emblem of Lilith, the Babylonian goddess of death. The owl is full of paradox, she notes: the purveyor of fertility and health for women in medieval Brittany and Saxony, the "bird that brings fear" in Cameroon and the deaths of children in Malaysia, and yet its hooting enunciates safety in Japan.

Infamously difficult to study, the owl carries the weight of many of our known unknowns as well as many more unknown unknowns. For all the contradictory associations humans have been ascribing to the owl over millennia, its uncanny hooting foils our attempt to pin down the meaning of the sign. The owl's call, in other word, renders us speechless.

While we wait out the gestational clock, we've been going about our regular lives, and it all feels surprisingly mundane. There's something of a "look at the birds of the air" simplicity to this second trimester season, which has surprised me.

Regardless of my anxieties and all the unknown unknowns of this child and our joint futures together, thinking too much about it all bears no good fruit. So, instead, I'm rushing to write before an extended sleeplessness draws a fog down over my small patch of draft work.

For much of this summer, I've relocated my morning writing to the side porch where I set up a makeshift plywood desk. Out here for a few hours each day, I've learned to greet the pair of tufted titmice who cycle through the skeletal branches of what is, as best I can figure out, an American Bladdernut. The titmice don't stay long, just turn their coxcomb heads about, squawk a few cycles, and then dip out, low and fast over the vine-covered fence. They don't seem to be nesting by the house, so I presume they flit back to feed their young somewhere in the forested creek below. What is clear is how hard they're working for their altricial chicks, born utterly helpless, featherless and blind.

Human infants are classified as "secondary altricial." Our babies are born as weak as featherless birds, with substantial postpartum development coming in the first few months, but ours are also, like foals and baby whales, precocial for the gestational energy we devote to a single progeny. Birds seem willing to lose an egg or two, given the odds, while orcas will mourn the death of their young for weeks, if not longer.

The other morning percher in this backyard tree is, oddly enough, a catbird. Titmouse and Catbird, as if trapped in some cartoon. They tolerate each other, but never on the same branch. One of the titmice is often here first but then yields the lowest branch when the catbird swings in, two inches bigger and sleek grey, with a long, svelte tail balanced by a thin, elongated beak. Silently, it holds the branch for a few minutes, and then they're both off, the bladdernut leaves fluttering in empty air.

These passerine birds need only a nest, a temporary place to house their young. These birds, they neither sow nor reap. Their seasonal home is just the general vicinity, this species-shared neighborhood, which includes me, mug-clasped man in mismatched shorts and sweater.

We are not the greater permanence here, they remind me. Perpetuity belongs to the roots of this giant silver maple and the old stones stacked into the foundation of this house. Our lives on branch and porch are much more provisional—claw-to-beak, as it were—and cyclical.

These dune hills, too, are vastly older and fundamentally strange. Just below the substrate, all over the wide cleft of this valley, sit the fossilized, three-toed imprints of dinosaur steps. In the 1830s, Edward Hitchcock, Professor of Natural Theology at Amherst College, collected thousands of such stone slabs from around the nearby villages of Greenfield and Turner's Falls. After meticulous study of the claw marks, he hypothized the prior existence of giant, flightless birds. He had no dinosaur bones to study just yet, only these trace effects of heavy, saurian foot-stepping. Imprints of absence.

Hitchcock's rock collection hangs now in the Berneki Museum in Amherst and tells a different story of the ground situation here. And in a strange way, the persistence of these prints grinds down some of my own anxieties as we lope our collective, heedless way deeper into the Anthropocene. There is urgent work to do, individual and societal actions to take, *in haste*. Yet, I'm convinced that speed alone will work to amend only one of our symptoms (namely, atmospheric warming) rather than the disease itself. Something more fundamental is at stake.

The environmental writer Fred Bahnson, riffing on Thomas Merton's question, "what can we gain by sailing to the moon if we are not able to cross the abyss that separates us from ourselves?" asks instead, "what can we gain by fixing climate change...if we remain alienated from ourselves?" How, in other words, do we tether our supposedly individual, free-floating selves back to the ground under our collective feet?

One response, urges Robert MacFarlane in *Underland: A Deep Time Journey,* involves looking down into the ground beneath us and looking back into the far reaches of geologic time. "When viewed in deep time," he writes, "things come alive that seemed inert. New responsibilities declare themselves. A conviviality of being leaps to mind and eye. The world becomes eerily various and vibrant again. Ice breathes. Rock has tides. Mountains ebb and flow. Stone pulses. We live on a restless earth."

Those claw-marked slabs of stone at the Berneki, housed alongside dinosaur skulls and an imposing mammoth skeleton, they time-stamp sandstone rock in a way that presses my 200-year worries into wonder.

We were awakened suddenly, back in late April, by the pulsing, proximate hooting of an owl. C. had just confirmed that she was pregnant again. The night air had turned decisively to spring, and we'd left the window open wide.

It wasn't obviously an owl at first. Pulled from the strange reaches of sleep, I thought some fenced dog was barking me back into consciousness. Or someone was calling up at us inexplicably. But when it hooted again, I sank back into the mattress, eyes wide in the dark.

"Do you hear that?" C. asked through a quiet exhalation of breath.

The repeated call hollowed out the frost-nipped air, vibrant and sonorous. It encircled the feet of the bed, crawled up across the bedspread and over our goose-bumped flesh. It repeated its urging, of aggression or love, I don't know, across an extended pitch-dark hour. The chirrups of a thousand insect wings went still as they yielded the edge air to this entity that had arrived.

The owl's recurrent hooting was crisp, like an apple, as sharp as an axe splitting hardwood. It struck in a way entirely opposite to the intermittent highway noise nearby: loud trucks hurtling through the sacrosanct night in a long swelling and recession of rubber clawing at asphalt. I cursed the combustion noise, fearing that the racket would drive off the owl.

But the call continued. Stay, I invited, as I tried to memorize the call. There was a spondaic questioning to the cycle, a two-part repetition with a difference. It had an extra, trailing hoot at the end. It was lonesome, imperial and singular.

Utterly alert, sleepless now, I traced my fingertips to my phone. In the funnel of indigo light, I searched for New England owls. On my second hit, I landed on a page dedicated to the barred owl where it's mnemonic call was transcribed as: who cooks for you? who cooks for you, all? Which was exactly the sound of the wordless question being urged from the trees behind the house.

For Thoreau this was "the most melancholy sound in Nature," the hooting owl. He heard in its "gurgling melodiousness" both "the dying moans of a human be-ing" and, with some distance in the woods, "only pleasing associations." Owls both terrified and soothed him. Their wild otherness caused him to state emphatically and plain-ly: "I rejoice that there are owls."

By now, C. had melted back into that first trimester sleep—long crests of inhalation descending into deep troughs of exhalation. The lungs of an oceanic womb. This child, I know, will be as stunning and as foreign to us as *strix varia* in the cry-split night.

Quietly, I padded down the stairs for a glass of water. The hooting seemed to follow me through the rental house. I was cold in bare feet by the kitchen sink, contemplating a quick step to the porch to see whether I could better guess its position, maybe see it by moonlight. I knew it was futile though, this urgency to *see*. Instead, I spent a few minutes with nose pressed to the screen above the counter. Chin cradled in upturned palms, I tried to conjure its unblinking eyes and wondered what it might mean, this sign in the night.

What is the point of an apparition, I wondered, if we can't know whether it offers a blessing or an omen?

But I've long since accepted that adulthood offers no fewer answers than childhood, that age does not necessar-ily consign wisdom, that the idea of home is too slippery an object to clutch. Simply holding one's palms open to the grief and the grace of this life seems enough.

I had only one thing to do: I climbed the stairs and crawled into the warmth of the sheets, burrowing back into a night humming with an unknowing as taut and as thin as the skin of the earth.

References

Andrew-Gee, Eric, "Bird Populations in Steep Decline in North America, Study Finds," *The Globe and Mail*, Sept. 14, 2016. https://www.theglobeandmail.com/technology/science/report-finds-north-american-skies-quieter-by-15-billion-fewer-birds/article31876053/ ͺ

Boulding, Elise, *Building a Global Civic Culture: Education for an Independent World*, Syracuse University Press, 1990.

Chaudhary, Ajay Singh, "It's Already Here: Left-wing Climate Realism and the Trump Climate Change Memo," *n+1*, Oct. 10. 2018, https://nplusonemag.com/authors/singh-chaudharyajay/.

Martone, Michael, *Unconventions: Attempting the Art of Craft and the Craft of Art*, University of Georgia Press, 2005.

MacFarlane, Robert, *Underland: A Deep Time Journey*. W.W.Norton, 2019.

Miles, Kathryn, "To Wit, to Woo: The Silence of Owls," Terrain.org. https://www.terrain.org/articles/24/miles.htm

Zimmer, Carl, "Birds Are Vanishing From North America," The New York Times, Sept 19, 2019 https://www.nytimes.com/2019/09/19/science/bird-populations-america-canada.html

Into the Bargain

Robert Miltner

The northeast Ohio sleet streaks and blurs the Christmas lights at the mall. Shapes of cars and pickups and vans in the parking lots look like snow-covered wrapping-papered presents. I'm circumnavigating the suburban mall in over-lapping loops, looking in the outlier locations where shoppers find low price specialties that fall outside the range of standard commercial fare.

This year it's called the Book Bazaar. Last year it was called Pop Up Paperbacks. The year before it was Holiday Hardback Flea Market. Another year it was the Close-Out Christmas Circus. The names change but the idea is the same: each is an impulse buyer's paradise for readers who look for good books at give-away prices.

Finding seasonal booksellers like Book Bazaar offers the joy of discovering new writers or old friends, and on a school teacher's salary. These are the Christmas presents I buy for myself. Residual traces of hunting and gathering intersect as I walk the aisles and book tables, alert and open to possibility.

Sometimes I find an amazing deal, like *Helen Frankenthaler: A Paintings Retrospective*, published in a coffee table hardback by Abrams and the Modern Art Museum of Fort Worth, which sells retail for seventy-five dollars but is marked down to a mere seven ninety-nine. The Frankenthaler was a close-out with a remainder mark slashed across the bottom of the book with a black Sharpie. I bought two copies when I found it, knowing I'd keep one for myself and give the other one to Alison, my artist daughter.

Somewhere in this temporary retail space leased for the holidays, this marina of docked tables, is the one table that holds books of poetry. From experience, I walk to the back and check the corner tables. Located just before the hallway that leads to the loading dock and the trash compactor, I find the poetry table.

This is where the book collector digs for treasure, in the area unexplored by the less impassioned; this is where I hope to find a first edition or a signed copy that has traveled the country after some bookstore shuttered its doors, a book now washed ashore and marooned on this table of poetry books. I hold my breath for a second as I arrive like a boat about to tie up to a pier.

I locate the small stacks of usual suspects. Robert Frost. Emily Dickinson. Edgar Allen Poe, though it's a collection of his stories. Anne Morrow Lindberg's *The Unicorn*. There's one Yeats, a Robert Penn Warren. And one hardback by someone named Raymond Carver. This name seems familiar. Haven't I read a short story of his? About some drunken couples swapping zany love stories? But this—*Where Water Comes Together with Other Water*—is a book of poetry.

The 1985 hardback edition with the dust jacket is in fine condition for being moved around in the brief years since its publication. And it's long for a book of poems, easily one hundred and thirty pages, twice the length of most poetry collections. The first poem, about Carver's first job at six-teen, stocking shelves at a Woolworth's retail store, evokes the memory of my first job at that same age, stocking shelves and delivering prescriptions for a local drug store in the small Ohio town where I grew up. In his final poem, about fishing but not catching anything, Carver writes, "At times I felt so happy I had to quit fishing." I recall that same feeling I'd had sitting on stone piers in Lake Erie where I fished when I was old enough to be alone, learning patience, and, like Carver, "listening to the sound the water made." Here is a poet writing lyrical narratives that reflect my current life's experiences in ways similar to his. The experience is new to me. As a writer myself, I appreciate how his poems succeed where mine fall short, how he catches fish while I cut bait.

But it's the title poem that grabs me by my shirtfront and won't let me go. "I'm 45 years old today," Carver writes, "Would anyone believe it if I said I was once 35?" I've nev-er encountered a poem before that addresses male mid-life transition. As a man barely in my forties, holding this book makes me feel like I'm outside a house and looking through the window and watching myself read. I stand in the Book Bazaar and read Carver's work straight through. I look back over some of the other poems, especially the ones about the water. I'm Carver's doppelgängered reader, entranced and transported.

I look across the store and through the glass windows to the parking lot outside. Cars have a layer of snow on their roofs, and large white flakes continue to fall and accumulate in the growing dark of the short winter day. I feel hungry, but I'm not sure what I'm hungry for. It's not a particular flavor or the difference between soup or sandwich. I do know that I need to eat something that will leave me feeling both full and sustained, for I have some vague task I must identify. I recall Hemingway saying that when he was hungry he would go to the museums in Paris to look at the art, and that being hungry made him a better writer. Has reading the Carver book made me want to write? Write better? Write right now? And if I do, will I feel satiated? Is this the kind of hunger I have?

Without thinking, I set down the book and leave the store. After I brush snow off the windshield of the car while it runs and warms up, I join the traffic flow of other workers driving home.

I'm eating dinner when I wonder why I didn't buy that book of poems by Raymond Carver. What was I thinking? Did my mind just drift elsewhere in the bookstore? Nothing unusual drew my attention. Walking away from the Carver book made me feel like I'd turned and walked away from a friend of mine who was telling me about some incident in his life and I just left in mid-sentence without even a goodbye. Am I in some way the friend himself, and this is some moment of meaning in my life and I had just walked out on myself? Perhaps something is missing, like the book itself, in my life? I need to know.

A powerful urge to hold the book in my hands and read it again, right at that moment, grips me. I feel paralyzed with embarrassment for foolishly walking away from something that held my attention so powerfully when it was in my hands. Away from it now, I feel impelled to jump up, grab my keys, and drive back to get it. The chance of the Book Bazaar still being open seems even more remote than the chance of a pop-up store having a land line to call. But even though I know this, I go anyway.

Twenty minutes later I'm standing in front of the closed store. The parking lot is empty except for my car. The December wind is brisk and insistent, cloying its way up my pant legs and coat sleeves, down my collar. In my haste I forgot my scarf and gloves. A Cleveland Indians baseball cap I found in the car, made of cotton, offers about as much protection for my head as a handkerchief. The winter wind makes a whistling sound as it chills my exposed ears so much that they sting.

I lean close to the glass. Though the store lights are out, I can see the back corner where the small table of poetry books are dimly lit by the low wattage exit sign. No nightlight ever seemed so sad. "Hello friend," I say out loud in the direction of the table of poetry books. "I'll be back tomorrow," I say to Raymond Carver, or the book of his poems, or to both. My cold right hand feels even colder fumbling for, then clutching the icy car keys. I turn the coat collar tighter, hunch up my shoulders, and begin my solitary walk back across the arctic expanse of the parking lot toward my car.

I'm restless and fidgety, finding it hard to get settled enough for sleep to come to me. Instead, I toss and turn and tumble in a lapidary of anxiety. Closing my eyes, I make myself recall the sound water makes in creeks, rivers, beaches. The lift and lull of moving water. The rhythm of waves like of breath slowing down to the calm farm pond of sleep.

When the alarm goes off in the morning I wake with

my head under a pillow. I call my high school, tell the secretary I'll be late but will get there by ten. This gives me time to stop at the Book Bazaar on my way to class.

I park the car, walk briskly across the windy expanse of the parking lot, scoot through the store's door, then move with purposeful speed toward the poetry table in the back of the store.

My joy of finding the Carver book still on the poetry table leaves me hyperventilating. I lift *Where Water Comes Together with Other Water* into the air as if it is a holy relic, clutch it briefly to my chest as if it is a prodigal child returned to the family. After packing it carefully for transport in my briefcase, I practically run to my car.

All day at school I obsess about the book. I have my students do in-class writing so I can reach into my desk drawer and touch it like it's a talisman or charm. During lunch break I stay in my classroom, looking at the cover, the Marion Ettlinger author photo on the back where Carver's arms and shoulders square into a partial frame. His fiery eyes look directly into mine, his gaze is challenging, his face as serious as the honesty of the poems he's written for this book.

The back of the book jacket is like a mirror in which I see myself. I recognize in the reflection my own immediate need as a writer to find the honesty to write this phase of my life. The challenge is clear. I breathe deep, exhale slowly, and accept finding myself living a moment where one poet's writing comes together with another poet's writing.

Outside, the shadows of parked cars and bare winter trees grow longer across the parking lot and lawns of snow.

Inside and seated at my faculty office desk, I feel alive in a way that allows me to fully experience this moment. Though I'm connected to another person, to another writer who I've met through a book, writing with common purpose, still I lack a vocabulary to express it.

Then something Carver writes in one of his poems comes to mind: "If this sounds like the story of a life, okay." It's as if he's telling me not to define or dissect or deconstruct everything. As if he's telling me that sometimes its best just to trust the way the story sounds, which is sometimes enough, even if I can't find the word to say it aloud.

I realize the book I've acquired has given me more than I bargained for. It is going to impact my life each time I read it over again, finding in successive readings not what is new in the book, but what I keep discovering about myself in each subsequent rereading. It's like when I was fifteen and read *Catcher in the Rye* for the first time, a book that traveled with me to college and beyond. Little is as thrilling as the gift of finding the right book at a significant time in one's life. If *Catcher in the Rye* was the book of my adolescence opening into my early adulthood, will *Where Water Comes Together with Other Water* be the book of my middle life transition? And why not? Caver's story is my story, too.

Looking up from my teacher's desk, I return my gaze to the wintery landscape outside my window. Change is coming to northeast Ohio. The shortest day of the year is nearly here. In incremental turns, the days will slowly grow longer, brighter, warmer. Snow will become sleet, sleet become rain, rain will bring another spring. A sense of movement bears me along as I merge this particular moment with a newly arriving stage of my life. I vow to trust the flow of the current.

Alice in Motherland

Vicky Oliver

I am a bad daughter. In my head, I am still sixteen years old, nursing all the hurts by myself like an orange tabby cat licking her wounds. The rocky road between me and my mother stretches back decades through perceived hurts and emotional minefields that (at least on my side) cannot be smoothed over. The time she took no interest in the publication of my first career book. The time she told me that being president of my University Club "didn't count," because the Club was virtual. The time she told me I could "do better" when it came to my choice of husband.

At 5 foot 9, I tower above her; my mother is five foot two on a tall day. But most of the time, I find myself stooping to her level. This makes me feel small, like a miniature Alice in Motherland.

Along with teacakes that say "Don't eat me or you'll get fat" and drinks that say "Don't drink me or you will spill it all over the white carpet," Motherland has rules that I don't understand. Whether or not I follow the rules, I'm still stuck there. One Christmas, about five years ago, the queen of Motherland (that would be my mother) had a screaming fit at the Harvard Club because I switched one of the place cards so that I could sit next to my husband. Was that so wrong?

When my first stepfather died, my mother, unprompted, put it like this: "I like you," (she said). "And you like me. But, we aren't close. When we see each other, we have a nice time." She made me sound like one of her acquaintances at her bi-weekly bridge game.

And yet, there is truth in what she said. We are not close, and when I see her, I have an okay time.

When she married my second stepfather, he told me that he was "horrified" that my relationship with my mother was so distant. We live but thirty blocks from each other in Manhattan. For all the times we get together a year, she may as well live in Timbuktu. He encouraged her to thaw toward me; and in turn, I reached down deep to try to thaw toward her—but by then all the hurts had congealed and hardened, and there was a lot of hard work to do, and most of the time I just didn't feel like it.

After all, what kind of a mother doesn't cheer on her daughter's accomplishments? Mine.

"Your mother is a piece of work," observed my friend Elizabeth after meeting her a few times.

My husband takes the opposite view. "She's always been hard on you, but now she's also cranky. You are not ten years old anymore. Grow up."

"Sixteen," I correct. "I am not sixteen."

"Okay." He laughs. "You are not sixteen anymore, and she's not a young woman." He sighs. "What are you going to do? She's the only mother you've got."

Is it stooping to her level to be miffed that she isn't nicer to me? Or more of a cheerleader? After all, I'm the only daughter she's got. And yet in a parallel universe where reason and rational thought prevail, I know that I cannot change her. I believe that people can only change if they genuinely want to. And even then, it's a crap shoot. She doesn't want to change. Therefore, any change in our dynamic must come from me.

Two years ago, she inadvertently hurt my feelings by ordering me to never again send her any sort of object for a present. My husband and I had just spent $300 on a set of gorgeous, hand-painted teacups from Bernaud for her for Christmas.

"She knows I love buying gifts, and she's taking away my one feeling of fun connected to her," I raged to my husband (who actually agreed with me). He and I loved the navy-blue teacups flecked with splashes of gold and had scrimped to buy them for her instead of us.

"Can't she just give them back to us?" he asked, scratching his head. "We'll be happy to take them off her hands."

Further, as she defined "objects," she also meant: clothing, gloves, jewelry, makeup, perfume, art, calendars, purses, shoes, and hats. Or any gift one might want to keep. Was I being childish to see this as a rejection of me? She was rejecting my gifts, after all. In a carefully worded email! (And copying her third husband on the communique.)

The Beatles once crooned, "You can't buy me love." Was I trying to buy her love? Why *was* I spending so much money on her gifts?

Last Christmas, I decided that the only consolation in not being allowed to buy her any personal gifts was that my husband and I could save a boatload of money (and then splurge on a gift for ourselves). For the first time, I forced myself to buy her the only thing I could think of that was not on her "don't buy me" list: flowers. I went to my local flower shop on East 51st Street and chose a purple orchid for $75. I wanted to also buy her a cactus since she's so prickly, but then I would blow my budget. I'd vowed that I would not spend real money on a transient gift. Included with the orchid, I wrote this note:

> Dear Mom,
> Merry Christmas. If you don't like this gift, please feel free to give it to your doorman, your maid, or some other deserving soul. No need to tell me about it!

When I told my husband about the note, he pleaded with me to return to the florist immediately and remove my note from the gift.

"Do not pass Go," he said.

"I've passed it," I said.

"No good can come of this," he said. "You're being petty. She doesn't mean to be as abrasive as she is."

"Well, she hurt me, and she doesn't even know it."

"You need to be the adult now," he said.

Dear God, say it isn't so. Wouldn't it easier to just stay in Motherland? It's frequently freezing there, and its rules make no sense, but at least I know the terrain. And with friends, sustenance, drinks like white wine that won't stain the carpet, and many sweaters, I can hang out there indefinitely.

And yet …

My husband is often right about emotional matters. And so, I actually went back to the florist. I got as far as the glass door. I stared inside at all the splendid orchids, lemon trees, and hydrangeas. In the twin glass cases along the back wall were all the roses and tulips in exotic colors. It was likely the only flower shop in Manhattan with purple tulips. The store was bursting with color, spring, music, rejuvenation. The store was teeming with love. I thought about my mother—the one who only "liked" me. Surely, I could reach down deep inside and forgive her. It was Christmas, after all.

Nah.

I am not taking the note off the orchid, I thought.

A few days later, she called me on the telephone.

"That was the perfect gift," she said. "Why would I ever give it to my doorman?"

Everything and the Kitchen Sink

Lea Page

I hate my kitchen sink.

No, really. I despise it. When I'm in the kitchen—and I'm not too fond of that, either—I avoid eye contact with the sink, as if it were a petty rival. I'm aware, deeply aware, of its deficiencies, and instead of politely overlooking them, I sneer when they are displayed. "Piece of shit," I say under my breath when I can't fit my mixing bowl under the faucet for a decent rinse. I sigh with unconcealed impatience at the anemic stream from the handheld sprayer.

The two little windows above the sink are shamefully inadequate. The sill outside is covered in mildew. The windows themselves are the kind that crank in and out, the kind that get stuck when I forget and open them more than six inches when I'm desperate for fresh air, for space, for something my eyes can safely settle upon. The biggest flaw with the windows is that they face north. Looking out of them is like reading with a dim bulb: my eyes alternately squint and widen in an effort to conserve and, at the same time, capture more light, a commodity which is in short supply in this land of grey and shrinking skies.

When people come over, they're not immediately horrified by the dark hole of my kitchen with its offending sink. "Oh, what a nice place this is," they say, as they take in the wide planks of pine on the floor, the fireplace and the built-in bookcases. They don't see what I see, and they have no concept at all of what desolation there is in what I don't see every time I step into this room.

My reaction might seem just a tad over the top. I *know* my reaction is over the top. But knowing that doesn't help me at all. This isn't really about the sink, of course. The real problem is that I can't see the horizon.

Montana, where we used to live, is defined not by its boundaries but by the lack of them. We measured distances by mountain range, and we were so much more aware of the four cardinal directions—north, south, east, west—because there was just so much more of each one. West was never just "that way."

For me, standing in my house, west was the pasture outside our living room windows where one spring, before the snow melted in the mountains, a moose gave birth to twins in the dry bed of the irrigation ditch. Farther west, the pasture stretched past our property line and ranged across the flat of the plain, interrupted only by cottonwood trees lined up single file along the sparse network of roads and ditches. Even farther west, the land lifted and plunged like the sea: green, brown or white, depending on the season, lapping up against the Absaroka Mountains and spilling beyond. Whole towns were hidden down in the troughs of the hills, which rolled on to the Gallatin Range. The city of Bozeman lay behind this, and more mountains. Finally, the western sun set after its long trip and hung suspended at the last moment for encore after encore of radiant sky. With a horizon like that, the only obstacles were the limits of my own imagination.

In New Hampshire, where we live now, I can't find the sun. Closed in by a wall of vegetation, I have lost my bearings. I mean, I know where I am. I can pull out a map and find it, right there: Canterbury, New Hampshire. Just a few miles east and north of Concord, the state capitol. But what does east mean anymore? Or north? The map tells me where Canterbury is in relation to everything else that is already here, but I need to know so much more than that.

We've been here for six months. At least, the three of us have: after we unloaded the U-Haul, our daughter Nina, about to begin her sophomore year in college, spent one night in the new house and then embarked on her own adventure. Meanwhile, I was pulling up carpet that reeked of cat piss. How had we missed that when we looked at the house with the real estate agent? Answer: all of our senses were dead at the time. We just needed a place, any place. I had forgotten how humid it is in the East and how much that magnifies the smell of things. At the risk of being overly dramatic, even the dirt here smells wrong to me, tinged with the scent of leaf mold and something else I can't put a finger on, as opposed to the clean, salty smell of alkali that I am used to.

Montana has the best weather, too, if you don't mind the cold. Even in the winter—especially in the winter—you have the same experience of vastness and penetrating light as you would on the ocean. At five thousand feet above sea level, the thin air is not only closer to the sun but seemingly holds more of it. The open space dwarfs anything with an upright posture. Even the Beartooth Mountains, jutting up from the high plain—no transition—just ten miles from our twenty-acre postage stamp of land, appeared much smaller than they were.

Recently, I was driving with our son Thomas on Highway 93, the artery out of Concord that takes you south to Boston, and I paused for a moment before pulling away from the tollbooth. There was no one behind us—New Hampshire does get its share of traffic, but relatively speaking, it is still a pretty rural state. "Just like Montana, isn't it?" people say, and we smile, pleased that they love their state so much and that they want us to love it, too. New Hampshire is, truly, a lovely state. But no, it is not just like Montana. In the same way that a baby can recognize, instinctively, the rhythm of its own mother's heartbeat or a mother can distinguish her child's voice in a crowd, Montana has made a permanent imprint on me: nothing else is quite like it.

In that moment before I put my foot on the gas, Thomas, fifteen, sighed and said, "It might sound crazy, but this toll plaza is my favorite place in New Hampshire."

"Mine, too," I said, and I gestured around, my hand taking in the way the highway expanded to fit the tollbooths and pushed back on the phalanxes of trees. "It's the only place you can see the sky."

It's not only the sun and sky that I miss, although I miss them with such a visceral longing, it frightens me.

177

The problem is not that I am having a hard time letting go of Montana. To use my husband's legal lingo, I will stipulate—admit right up front—that I *am* having a hard time letting go, of Montana and of my dream for our life there: a family, a home, a garden, a community.

In Montana, when I stood at my sink in the kitchen, a room whose design I had sketched on a piece of graph paper, starting with my grandmother's wooden kitchen table and drawing out from there, I would leave the window cracked open in the spring, even though it was often chilly. I had planted a crabapple tree right beside that window. Not so close that I couldn't see the sky behind it pinking at dawn, but close enough that I could hear the honeybees when they came. It's a wonder that the whole tree wasn't lifted into heaven by the bees, so many were drawn to its blossoms.

But the number of bees on our tree camouflaged the fact that honeybees as a species are struggling to survive. I've read that in order to comprehend why, we must understand that the smallest unit capable of living is not the single bee, but the whole hive. The colony is a single organism. The bee, alone, cannot live. It is also said that we humans cannot survive without a human community. Like the bees, we thrive when surrounded by the warmth and industry of human companionship.

I've always associated bees with the purest form of light and joy. They communicate by dancing and turn the sun into liquid gold. That they are a model of community seems a given. But consider: a colony of bees is ruled by a queen who lives in darkness. When she first hatches, she must eat her sisters, who, by virtue of their latecomer status, must sacrifice their bodies to provide the queen

178

the extra protein she needs to become the grotesquely large being who gives new life to the hive and ensures its future. There can be ugliness—violence even—behind the most outwardly peaceful and cooperative of natural communities. A strict code of behavior. An unquestionable hierarchy. You must accept your place or fight for a new one, and some individuals—outliers—may be sacrificed for the sake of the integrity of the group. It is the natural order of things, and, as we learned first-hand, it can be brutal.

I had a dream that my family would belong in a tiny, seemingly friendly town in a magnificently beautiful place. That didn't happen. When dreams die, you have to find a way to let them go—with grace, if you're lucky—but you have to release them, even if the doing of it is awkward, or even ugly, as it is for me. Otherwise, the dream becomes regret, which will destroy any beauty your memories hold, the equivalent of following your dream to its grave.

Right now, that is what I am in danger of doing, less than a year after leaving. Yes, I remember the bullying of our daughter in her school, the ostracism—we remained outsiders—and the silence and the denial, and those are not easy memories. I still have to consciously suppress a shudder when I breathe in the memory of my daughter's eyes, dull and downcast in despair, and I have to will my jaw to unclench when I breathe out the memory of so many faces feigning innocence. But the good memories of our fifteen years in Montana—of the beauty of the landscape, of the unexpected generosity of a neighbor, of the reassuring rhythm of our family suppers, which were quiet always for just a moment with the candle being lit and then raucous afterward because no one can suffer my husband Ray's deliciously terrible jokes and puns in silence—those memories make letting go even harder.

I wake up at night now—I wake up *every* night—with the low ceiling of our New England Cape angling close to my head, and the questions come: Should we have stayed? A local Montana author once published a book about what it took to make it in a small town. Are you that kind of person, the title asked or maybe just implied—I might have been feeling a bit defensive. Maybe I should have bought it. But what would the author, a childless single man, be able to tell me about running the gauntlet of school, playground and swimming pool when my daughter was among the first, if not *the* first—certainly the first child in her class—to arrive from out of state? For all I know, it was a joke book, but for me, it wasn't a laughing matter. Maybe that was the problem. Did I just overreact and drive us from our home?

When my rational mind has a slim upper hand, daytime mostly, but not always even then, I counter those questions with another: how could we possibly have stayed? And then Ray will come out of the study that he has turned into a makeshift office, and he will pull the heaviness in his face up into an unconvincing smile. He gives it his best effort, but his skin is grey, and the crow's feet beside his eyes don't do their normal dance. He's faking it for my sake—he is just as devastated as I am—and that only makes me love him more, but each time he does it, I stagger a moment before I can balance the new load of guilt.

I admit this to Ray one night when my thrashing wakes him. In the dark—I can't see out our tiny window, and

I've lost track of the moon—I tell him that I am afraid we have made a grave mistake in leaving Montana, that it is all my fault, that I have destroyed what we had for no good reason. I can hear the shrug in his voice as he says, "Every plant needs to be repotted now and then."

But what does *he* know about plants? A year before we left Montana, when Nina was home for the summer, I sent her to Ray's office one day with directions to take care of the houseplant that stood in the corner of his office by the door.

"Mom sent me here to take care of your plant," she said when she arrived, and Ray got up from his desk to show her where to find the plant food and watering can.

"No, Dad," she said, and she lowered her chin and her voice and looked at him from under her brow, "not *that* kind of take care."

The plant was almost entirely dead, all crinkly brown leaves except for one that had a hint of green along its center rib. Ray is optimistic by nature and would have kept on watering and feeding and feeding and watering. It is quite possible that the plant would have choked along for years. In fact, it already had, but I—a pessimist? A real-ist? The jealous queen of fairy tales?—I sent my daughter with a death warrant, and she turned the plant out into the dumpster in the alley and brought me the empty pot as proof of her deed.

It seemed necessary at the time, and I had always trusted my instincts when it came to growing things. I would tend them with love and tenderness, while also acknowl-edging the reality that sometimes you have to be ruthless, cutting back or thinning or pulling up a finished or dying plant by the roots to make room for something new. Now,

I am so ensnared between the iron jaws of my dream—the trap of the future—and of my regret over how things turned out—the trap of the past—that I no longer trust my instincts or my perceptions. My thoughts hound me like Harpies. Did we really have to go? Could I have done things differently? But I can't run from those questions the way I ran from Montana. I can't run from *myself* the way I ran from Montana.

The task before me now is to look out of this kitchen window in New Hampshire, not in search of the beauty that I used to see or wish I still saw, but simply, to see. To see the plain truth of what *is* because that is the only ground in which what *might be* can take root.

My Rock

Rhonda J. Ray

Early morning sunlight streamed through the bedroom window, and I awoke blinking, listening to pots and pans clanging in the kitchen. I lay still, shutting my eyelids tight against the light. But my eyes opened wide when my sister Linda, almost fourteen, stepped on me as she scrambled from her side of the bed against the wall to the edge of the mattress and to the floor.

"Hey, watch out!" I frowned. I was eight and slept on the outside of the bed because she was afraid to sleep next to the window.

"It's time to get up anyway to get ready for church," she said. "You too, Shannon."

Our five-year-old sister rolled over in her bed across the room, and Linda donned a robe and went out, shutting the door behind her. I couldn't make out her muffled words, but I knew everyone's Sunday morning routine. "Here. Bring it back when you're done, and keep the pages together, damn it," Daddy said, as he sat on the couch reading the Sunday *News & Observer*.

Linda reentered, carrying parts of the paper, and

clambered back to her side of the bed, rattling newsprint. When she finished the comics, she passed them to me and then turned to the society pages, her favorite section. She scrutinized the bridal photos and details of the wedding dresses, attendants, reception, and honeymoon.

I chuckled at *Blondie* and *Dennis the Menace* and studied the latest adventure of *Prince Valiant*. By the time I finished the comics, the aroma of bacon, which Mama cooked on Sunday mornings only, made my stomach growl, and I got up to eat and dress for Sunday school.

Pleasant Grove Baptist Church stood a few hundred yards up the road from where we lived in rural North Carolina. Almost every Sunday in the nineteen-sixties, my sisters and I walked there and back beneath our neighbors' pecan trees that lined the shoulder of the road. We trod grass and weeds in spring and summer, leaves and frozen ground in fall and winter.

Daddy visited church only for a rare funeral or rarer wedding, but he never tried to stop his children from attending. "Damned hypocrites" he called churchgoers. He got along with his neighbors, but religion or church attendance was not something he had in common with most of them. His mother had tainted his views about church. When he was a youth, she had prioritized her church community over her family and had been unavailable and remote as mother and wife.

Mama almost never went to church, although she was a church member. Her father, she said, didn't allow her to go to worship services when she was young, so when she married Daddy and moved next door to a church, she committed her life to Jesus and was baptized.

Although she liked church, Mama preferred to spend

Sunday mornings preparing big meals for her family. She started cooking soon after breakfast, and we ate at about two o'clock in the afternoon. After returning from church, I helped set the table, fill glasses with ice for sweet tea, and place food on the table. "Come and eat," Mama called when the feast was ready. She beamed as her family gathered around the table, eying the plate of fried chicken, bowls of mashed potatoes, green beans, field peas, and turnip greens, along with hot biscuits and made-from-scratch chocolate cake. These Sunday dinners, our best meals of the week, required hours to make. Besides, Mama spent time with God in the fields and woods and talked with Him most anytime.

My two brothers used to go to church but had stopped, maybe following Daddy's lead. But Linda, Shannon, and I attended Sunday school regularly, arriving clean, scrubbed, and wearing our best dresses that Mama had ironed as part of her Saturday night routine.

Before we departed, I approached my father. "Daddy, can we have some money for the offering?" I asked without fear or anxiety. He never refused this request. Reaching into his pocket, he pulled out some coins and selected three pennies, one for each of us. It was a small mite but more than he could well afford and probably more than he wanted to give.

The church, built of red brick with white trim, featured a wide porch. We entered through wooden doors opening into a vestibule and then passed through inner doors into the sanctuary. Stained glass windows on the outer walls displayed scenes such as Jesus holding a lamb, kneeling in prayer in the Garden of Gethsemane, and being baptized by John the Baptist. On bright days, sunlight flooded the sanctuary with red, purple, blue, and gold light that made the room appear otherworldly.

As Daddy instructed, we walked facing passing vehicles, but we usually arrived early to avoid most of the church traffic. In the winter, we were among the first inside the building, along with Mr. Carroll, who drove to the church to light the gas heaters in the sanctuary. With our coats on, we stood near the heaters rubbing our hands together as we waited for the space to warm. My sisters and I had known the people of this church all our lives, but we never said much as we waited for Sunday school to begin.

"How are you girls doing this morning?" Mr. Carroll asked.

"Fine," one of us answered, face flushing red. Polite but shy, we rarely initiated conversation with our elders.

Soon, we sat down in the oak pews, and Sunday school began. The minister and Mr. Carroll, who led the music with his deep bass voice, entered from the back, along with the choir members, who filed into rows behind the pulpit. The pianist played, and we all sang hymns such as "When We All Get to Heaven," "What a Friend we have in Jesus," and "Leaning on the Everlasting Arms." Racks attached to the back of the pews held hymnals and paper fans. During the summer, the congregation swished the fans back and forth on faces glowing with sweat.

I loved to sing these old hymns. Their words encouraged and inspired me, and the melodies uplifted me, making me want to soar. Sometimes, one of these familiar hymn drifts into my consciousness. I may not recall all the words, but I hear the tunes and am transported across time and space, singing again with even more joy than I felt then.

Sunday school consisted of a brief period of announcements, prayer, and song. Then we went to our classes, where we studied our Bible lessons. On Saturday nights, my sisters and I prepared by reading each week's lesson, published in small magazines called quarterlies. Worship services took place after Sunday school, and I began staying to hear the pastor's sermon when I was about eleven, old enough to focus and not fidget.

My first recollection of Sunday school was when I was promoted to the junior girls' class. One fall Sunday when I was six, someone came to my preschool class to escort me to my new classroom. Mrs. Lee taught the junior girls, ages six through eleven. Wearing spectacles and short, gray hair curled by a perm, she stood at a podium to lead us in our Bible study. Sometimes, she sang solo renditions of *Rock of Ages* and *Amazing Grace*. Her voice cracked, but I admired her knowledge of all the words to all the verses. Mrs. Lee taught the junior girls, including my sisters, for many years. Other than my mother, she was the person who most influenced my relationship with Christ when I was a child.

I hadn't minded my small offering when I was six, but now that I was eight, I pretended to be nonchalant when I handed in my envelope containing my penny in the junior girls' class. I glanced away from the class secretary, an older girl, who counted it along with others' nickels, dimes, and quarters to take to the church financial secretary.

When we returned to the sanctuary for dismissal of Sunday school, I usually sat by myself unless I sat with one of my sisters. The people at church knew Daddy's eccentricities, drove past our house with its peeling paint, and craned their necks to observe us when we walked to and from church. I couldn't seem to escape embarrassment and shame even in the house of the Lord. But I tried not to dwell on my feelings. After all, I liked going to church, and I wanted to learn about Jesus and follow him. I wanted to know a loving Father.

The summer I turned nine, the sun's early morning rays shone bright and hot as I stood waiting by the mailbox for Martha Ann, my father's cousin, to pick me up. She had invited me to Bible School at Mt. Zion, the Methodist church she attended about eight miles away. I held my Bible, a Christmas present from Mama, purchased at the dime store in the nearby town of Fuquay. As I waited, I turned to the first chapter of Genesis. I had never before taken the initiative to read the Bible on my own, and new worlds, new discoveries opened for me.

Each summer, I attended Bible school at my own church and looked forward to these week-long events. I stood with other children on steps leading to the pulpit to sing "Deep and Wide," stretching my hands up and down and rippling my fingers to illustrate "a fountain flowing in my soul." The sanctuary echoed "This Little Light of Mine," and I held up my forefinger in lieu of a shining candle. I munched cookies and sipped iced Coke and crafted gifts for Mama—one year, a lop-sided wooden cutting board and, another year, a picture of pink dogwood blossoms polyurethaned on stained wood. In Bible school, I memorized my first scripture, John 3: 16. "For God so loved the world that he gave his only begotten son, that whosoever believeth in him shall not perish, but have everlasting life."

When Mama and Daddy agreed that I could visit another Bible school, I jumped at the chance. I had no idea how much an unexpected event there would affect me.

Several of my classmates from school attended this church and Bible school, and all week, I enjoyed spending time with them. On the last day, my class filed into the sanctuary, and the minister began speaking to us. My thoughts wandered, and when I looked up, I noticed my classmates moving to the front of the church. Arising from my seat, I followed and knelt with them. I didn't know what had happened—didn't realize they were professing a commitment to Christ and consequently to the church. When I understood my mistake—not in my feelings towards Christ but in making a commitment to this church at this time, I was too embarrassed to say anything and got swept along by unfolding events.

I saw the consequences of my cowardice when the preacher visited my home to speak to my father. As I watched from the kitchen window, the pastor got out of his car and walked towards Daddy, who was already outside. I hadn't expected this visit. My heart raced. How did I get myself in such a mess?

I can only imagine their conversation, but Daddy told the pastor that I couldn't be baptized nor become a member of a church so far from home. As mortified as I felt about this situation, I was relieved. My declaration of faith that day had been accidental, and I was too afraid to admit my error. I hadn't explained to anyone what had really happened at the time, and I didn't set the record straight now either.

Two years passed, and my commitment to Christ came to a trial when I was almost eleven. That summer, my church had a revival. Every night for a week, a visiting preacher offered hope of salvation and grace as paper fans swished back and forth in hopes of stirring a small breeze. I attended the revival with my mother and Linda. At the close of an impassioned sermon near the end of the week, the preacher issued the traditional invitation to members of the audience to commit their lives to Christ: "If you are ready to surrender your life to Jesus and let him be your Lord, then come."

As the pianist quietly played the invitational hymn "Just as I Am" and the audience sang softly, Linda rose from her seat and stepped across me to get to the aisle. At sixteen, in a light blue dress and low heels, she paced towards the front of the sanctuary, head erect and eyes straight ahead. She had followed Christ for years and wanted to make her dedication public. When she reached the visiting minister and our pastor, who stood by his side, she leaned forward and said something, and our pastor responded in low tones.

As I continued singing the words of this hymn, I felt an overwhelming urge to join her. I left my pew and walked to the front of the church without hesitation. I too wanted to commit my life to Christ.

After the service, I stood beside Linda as church members came up to greet us and welcome us into the congregation. I received their outstretched hands with elation. If Linda objected to my following her, she never said. But whatever she thought soon wouldn't matter.

I didn't anticipate Daddy's response. In the next few days, the pastor of our church visited to talk to our father about his daughters' decision. Daddy didn't object to Linda's being baptized and joining the church, but he thought I was too young to take this step. He didn't think I knew what I was doing. I'm sure he recalled the previous incident. He refused to let me be baptized.

I was devastated. Two years earlier, I made a child's error because I was distracted and not paying attention. I was responsible for that mistake. Then, I didn't object to my father's interference. In fact, I was grateful. Now, I made a conscious and personal decision that affected my soul and my mind. I loved Christ and made this commitment publicly and privately. My father's interference felt like a violation of my very being.

Daddy's tyranny hurt me many times, but this time felt the worst. I could hardly believe his attitude, taking my decision out of my hands. I felt helpless, upset, traumatized, and crushed in spirit. Disagreeing or getting mad with my father never helped. He always won. The feeling of powerlessness in the face of such oppression felt unbearable.

I wept, suffering in silence. I didn't talk to Daddy about the matter, nor did he talk to me. Discussion was not his way. He reigned supreme in his household and always thought he knew best. I'm sure he thought such decisions were his to make, that he was even protecting me.

Linda's baptism was performed at a local pond in the area. Our pastor dipped her into the water, and when she emerged, she was a new creature in Christ symbolically and publicly. On the morning of Linda's baptism, I could not bring myself to go. I felt too much pain and rejection from my father and, to a degree, from God. Linda didn't seem to care if I got baptized or not. Daddy's decision about me didn't affect her. As siblings, we all cared about one another, but when Daddy yelled at one of us or caused pain, we kept our heads down, troubled but unwilling to challenge him.

In the coming weeks, despite my grief and embarrassment, I returned to church. Mrs. Lee talked to me privately and expressed sorrow over what had happened. Others reached out to me with kindness. Their sympathy only made me feel worse. People pitied me, but no one could understand how I felt. I continued to be a believer, but my heart could not overcome its trauma.

I knew God had not abandoned me, but I had to find solace so that I could begin to heal. The farm had acres of woods filled with pine trees, dogwood trees, sassafras trees, persimmon trees, hickory trees, wild gooseberries and blackberries, and other undergrowth that caught at my clothing and scratched my arms and legs. The woods surrounded the fields, from which barely visible paths led into the trees and bushes. I started spending time walking, past the tobacco barns, past the pond, heading to the back field, far from the house, out of sight. I entered the woods and found a place of refuge. It was a concave space in the ground where a pine tree had fallen, its roots sticking straight up in the air, pointing towards heaven.

For years, I sat in this depression in the ground and contemplated my life. I lay back and watched the wind moving in the pine trees waving above me, welcoming me, uttering a language all their own. I again found peace and God's presence. I believed God understood. He knew my problems and the reasons I could not again face baptism. Whenever I thought of this painful episode, I quickly put it out of my mind, beginning a habit of avoiding whatever might create or open deep wounds. I decided that God wouldn't care whether I was baptized or not. And so I wasn't—not for another twenty-five years.

Blue Heaven

Claude Clayton Smith

In my earliest memory I am scrambling up a ladder behind my older brother. I can't be more than two or three years old, because I turned four soon after we moved to Stratford. But this is Oakdale Manor near Lake Zoar, the long ladder rising into a cloudless blue sky. It is propped at a steep angle against the side of a one-car garage that my father is building, beside a small Cape Cod house that he also built, just after I was born. My father and grandfather are perched high on the peaked roof of that garage, tacking down tar paper in preparation for shingling. The *bang-bang-bang* of their hammers echoes around the low hills of Oakdale Manor, hills dense with more pine than oak—tall white pines my father planted as seedlings when *he* was a kid. When a country acre in that corner of Connecticut cost but a dollar.

Now my brother gains the top rung of the ladder and crawls up the bare plywood roof on his hands and knees. But I'm afraid to follow. *What on earth are you doing up there?* my mother shouts from below. She is holding an infant in her arms, her third child—another son—our new baby brother. I look down but it's a mistake. All I can see is the top of my mother's head, a bird's eye view that gives me vertigo. *Hold on!* my father cries. Then he works his way over to the ladder and carries me safely down.

Meanwhile, seated high on the roof, my brother hugs his knees and laughs.

To find Oakdale Manor you must take the old Connecticut Route 25 north to Newtown, turn right at the huge flagpole in the middle of Main Street, and descend the long hill into Sandy Hook, a one-horse crossroads of Grain & Feed stores. Turn left at the blinking yellow light and follow the winding blacktop road through the forested corridor that follows. Tucked into the trees by a long pond off the left is a brick structure the size of a big doghouse, the property of the local hydraulic company that owns the pond. This, according to my grandfather, was the brick house built by the Three Little Pigs, the only one to survive the Big Bad Wolf.

Minutes later the road reaches Lake Zoar, a narrow body of water formed by a dam on the Housatonic River. The old iron bridge that spans the lake at that point seems made from an Erector Set, its girder-like beams crisscrossing high overhead between sides shaped like the protractors we'd come to know in grammar school. As a boy my father used to jump from that bridge—a drop of thirty feet or more, straight down, feet first, one hand cupped about his crotch—a feat that my brothers and I never tried to duplicate.

Painted silver, the bridge forms a T with the road on the far side of the lake, and a right turn points you toward

Oakdale Manor. Before long you pass a ramshackle tavern called *Toot-'n'-Come-In*, my grandfather's favorite watering hole. Then *keep your eyes peeled*, as my father would say, for a quick left turn—a dirt road that curls up and over a set of railroad tracks and drops down-with-a-bump into the heart of another world.

Oakdale Manor, as I knew it, was a small, horseshoe-shaped valley. *Glen* conveys the smallness better but is simply too pastoral a term. The place was never green or lush but ragged with sandy crabgrass and scrubby weeds. Except for the Ditters' yard. The Ditters had a lawn. The lone street, White Birch Lane—a narrow strip of worn asphalt—sloped gently downhill from our house for a hundred yards or so to a dead end at the bottom of the horseshoe. Higher up, a pine-filled ridge ran the length of the overhanging hills, shading the railroad tracks by the narrow entrance at the crest of the U. Had I been able to follow my brother up the garage roof that day, Oakdale Manor would have spread out below me like a rustic village in a fable:

Our house, a wooden frame with white clapboard siding, is first on the left at the top of the lane. My grandparents' screened-in summer cottage squats next door, farther back from the edge of the road, on an earth-and-pine-needle floor. Half a dozen enormous white pines stand behind it, as if they had strayed from their relatives on the ridge. The home of Hill and Mae Larson—an elderly couple—sits third on the left, a boxy, added-on-to house, with tall pines and white birch at random out front. It draws its water, like all homes in Oakdale Manor, from an artesian well that my grandfather dug.

The Ditters live across from the Larsons in a long ranch house that sports a picture window in a fieldstone wall. A single row of whitewashed rocks separates their lawn from the edge of the road. A thick metal chain, slung low between two cedar posts, guards their gravel driveway. I loved to run my hand along the smooth links of that heavy chain. And those cedar posts were just my size. But even today, whenever the Ditters are mentioned, I get a queer sense of them clustered down there behind a barrier more forbidding than that chain—apart from Oakdale Manor— shut off from a place that was in itself shut off. And so when Oakdale Manor was the only world I knew, the Ditters occupied the most remote corner of it.

Old Man Ditter I rarely saw, his wife more rarely so. There was a pimply son called Frankie, and an older daughter who was always off somewhere. Frankie often regaled us with tales of hitchhiking all the way to Sandy Hook, a daring journey to the very ends of the earth. And my grandfather once told us of Old Man Ditter going to court with cow dung on his boots, which he wiped on the rung of a chair when the judge found him guilty of something-or-other. Whereupon the judge promptly doubled his fine.

I can recall no other homes. No, I vaguely remember a house in the woods beyond the Larsons', halfway up the steep hill where White Birch Lane abruptly ended. And there may have been a trailer in the open lot across from my grandparents' cottage that belonged to Henry Barnes, my father's boyhood friend. Or maybe it was Gibby and Olive's. Gibby was Reggie's brother—Reggie often played guitar to my father's banjo at Toot-'n'-Come-In—and Olive,

Gibby's wife, was said to have been in love with my father. But I think that trailer, if it ever existed, belonged to the Barnes, put there after Henry had to marry Ethel. Then Reggie set up his first wife with her lover in a motel room, so he could obtain a divorce and marry Muriel. But all of these dwellings and soap-opera shenanigans go up in smoke as fast as my memory constructs them. Oakdale Manor was a misnomer. The place made no claim to nobility.

And that was the extent of my childhood territory, a pleasant-enough expanse of scruffy earth not much bigger than a football field. As good a place as any in which to begin.

There were no playmates except my brother, who was fifteen months older. My mother once sent me to a birthday party dressed as a girl in a yellow dress, with a matching yellow ribbon in my hair. Apparently, it was the fashion in those days to dress little boys as girls, regardless of what Freud might have said—my mother, who would later bear a fourth son, had always wanted a little girl—but I can't imagine whose party it was, or who the other children might have been. I can only remember my intense embarrassment and hot tears of shame. And I'm sure my brother had a good laugh.

But all such moments were quickly forgotten when we went riding down White Birch Lane in our black metal wagon, an old Radio Flyer with a long handle like that of a snow shovel. I never got to steer, of course, but rode tucked behind my brother, knees out, arms around his waist. One day, as we careened along, I turned my head just in time to see the right rear wheel begin to wobble. I saw it happen in slow motion and knew that we would crash. My brother had no warning—which is probably why he doesn't recall the incident—but the wheel spun off, the axle sparked along the asphalt, and we tumbled into the middle of White Birch Lane. It must have been summer because we were wearing short pants. Our hands and knees were badly skinned, and we cried all the way to the Mercurochrome.

But my brother *does* remember a more serious incident that involved another wagon, the kind that came with wooden side-rails. It belonged to the Larsons' grandchildren, who often visited in the summer months. On this particular day the side-rails had been removed, and the metal joints into which they had been inserted were sharp and rusty:

My brother is standing in the wagon, holding court, when the wagon suddenly moves and he loses his balance. Falling out, he slices his calf to the bone on one of the naked metal joints. There is a moment of silence, then a trickle of blood along the length of the slice. A crimson torrent follows. My brother makes a funny noise and starts awkwardly home. But I don't assist him. I don't do anything. I am paralyzed with fear.

Or maybe I think it's funny to see him hobbling away, because I find myself laughing, just as he laughed at me from the top of the garage roof. Then a neighbor magically materializes with an open Jeep, and my brother—sitting on my mother's lap with a bloody rag wrapped about his leg—is whisked off to Dr. Iggy's office on the long hill above Sandy Hook, returning hours later after a tetanus shot and twenty-nine stitches. To this day he is bothered by cramps in that leg. And I am bothered by the memory of my laughter.

Strangely, I can't remember the interior of our home at Oakdale Manor, just as I recall nothing of the winter months.

New England winters being what they are, we must have spent them indoors. Yet I can see neither the inside of our house nor snow on the ground without. Mostly, our days were spent waiting for my father to come home from work. He commuted all the way down Route 25 to the General Electric plant in Bridgeport, a ride of well over an hour. In winter the drive was treacherous. Tire chains were needed just to get out the driveway, up White Birch Lane, and over the ridge by the railroad tracks. My father wouldn't get home until long after dark—long after we had been put to bed—only to be up and out again at five-thirty in the morning. So in winter we saw him only on weekends. That was one reason why we moved to Stratford, plus the fact that my mother, who had been born in New York City and raised in Bridgeport, had no love for the country. But building a house in Oakdale Manor had been my father's dream, and he did so soon after they married.

Three dramatic events took place within that house, the sketchy details of the interior notwithstanding—my father killed a bat with a broom, my parents found hornets crawling in the sheets of their bed, and the pressure cooker exploded in the kitchen. The images are stark and brief: my father holds up the ugly bat by its wingtips, my mother runs screaming from an upstairs bedroom in her pajamas, and the kitchen ceiling drips with soft, pale beans. Still, although these incidents took place within our home, the interior does not come into focus.

The front porch, however, a small cold square of concrete, remains clearly in my mind. It is there I stood crying loudly—pounding on the screen door that for some reason was locked—after running home from the birthday party to which my mother sent me dressed as a girl. Beyond that porch, a flagstone walk led to an arched rose trellis at the very edge of White Birch Lane, the gateway to our humble estate. And from the center of that arched trellis hung a wooden sign that my father had made, shiny with lacquer and sawed in rustic angles at both ends, like the kind you find at country souvenir shops. Wood-burned in simple script, it said *Blue Heaven*.

Holidays brought excitement to Oakdale Manor, especially the Fourth of July. Suddenly roadside fireworks stands— long since illegal in the state—popped up everywhere, with their star-spangled packages of splendor and noise. As soon as it was dark, with the lightning bugs as an opening act, we would walk up the road to the railroad tracks at the crest of the ridge, and the local men would shower the night with colorful bursts and flashes, to the thin accompaniment of *ooh*'s and *aah*'s. Skyrockets were launched from short sticks, Roman candles belched like mortars from wide-mouthed milk bottles, and my brother and I waved sparklers, inscribing bright circles in the black shadows of the pines:

One year a group of older boys, led by Frankie Ditter, are able to buy firecrackers, and I somehow get old of a one-incher—not as formidable as a fat red two-incher, but enough bang for any small boy. Stealing into the Larsons' side yard with a fistful of my grandfather's stick matches, I light the small bomb, throw it down, and plug my ears. I wait, but nothing happens. After a few long seconds, as I bend down sideways to investigate, the firecracker explodes and my right ear rings. In my fright I run into the back yard where the adults are seated around a picnic table, singing along to my father's banjo and Reggie's guitar. But I can't hear the music. Someone says something to me and I shrug my shoulders. Eventually, to my enormous relief, the ringing subsides, and I never touch another firecracker again.

There was another kind of fireworks as well. Late one night, awakened by the clanging of the volunteer fire department, my father roused my brother and me and brought us outside on the front porch to watch, joined moments later by my mother and baby brother. The sky was streaked in red above the woods behind the Ditters' place, the smoke barely visible, a red glow the only sign of fire. Then a siren screamed at the railroad tracks and a fire engine flew by White Birch Lane, following a dirt road along the ridge and out of sight. In the morning all talk in Oakdale Manor was of the fire. It had begun in someone's cellar and razed the bungalow above it. And in every conversation a strange laughter could be heard, different from the kind of laughter my brother and I often exchanged at each other's expense. The fire had been caused by an exploding still. And the fire engine that roared past our house that night returned every year on Christmas Eve to park in the vacant lot across the street. Santa Claus sat in the driver's seat, a spotted Dalmatian at his side. Our expectant faces shone like Christmas candles in the cold darkness. I recall the sparse crowd of neighbors, the huge sack on the seat between Santa and his dog, and a small Christmas gift for everyone.

Finally, there was the cove.

It cut in from Lake Zoar around the corner from White Birch Lane on the other side of the ridge. It was about forty yards wide, perhaps eighty yards long and, like the ridge, horseshoe-shaped. The woods grew right to its edge. There was a narrow dock at the end of the footpath that began where the ridge road ended, and I loved to bounce up and down on its slatted boards, testing the buoyancy of the barrels beneath. We never had a boat, although the rotting hull in the tall grass beside the barn-like boathouse was from a dinghy that had belonged to my grandfather.

A short stretch of sandy beach lay to the left of the dock, and a few trees had been cleared along the shore, making room for one or two blankets. To this spot my father would take my brother and me, with a huge black inner tube and a length of clothesline. We took turns on that tube, floating in the middle of the cove, arms and legs splashing, the sharp nozzle occasionally sticking us in the ribs. My father would tie the rope to a skinny birch on the bank, and if we lay still enough the rope would begin to sink. When it was my turn I could never relax, afraid that my father would wander from his post. I was always checking the rope, checking its white, wavy descent beneath the surface. The lake proper loomed on my right, a long and darksome body of water that seemed to lead right out of existence. The clotheslines was an umbilical cord—the cove a womb—and I clung to it steadfastly, not at all ready for the wide world beyond.

I never enjoyed floating in the cove. It was just something we did. And whenever black clouds rushed overhead, sprinkling the surface with circular *bloops*, my father would haul in the clothesline hand over fist, and we'd hurry home to watch the summer storm from the porch of my grandfather's cottage. I would press my nose to the dirty screen, watching the pelting rain, and for the rest of the day my nose would bear a dark smudge like the kind I would one day receive on my forehead on Ash Wednesday. I would recoil at the rumble of thunder, and my grandfather would laugh and say, *The Coal Man's coming!* The rending lightning, for which no explanation was ever offered, silenced me too.

Such was life in Oakdale Manor.

Returning there once after an absence of four decades, I realized that the cove was not a cove but the mouth of the Pomperaug River where it enters Lake Zoar. So much for memory. And I discovered that James Thurber had lived in Sandy Hook while we were living on White Birch Lane. Ed Sullivan had had a home in the vicinity, too. But in those days I couldn't even read. And we didn't get our first television set until we moved to Stratford.

From the shelter of my father's Blue Heaven.

4 Generations of Black Hair Matters

Marsha Lynn Smith

As my toddler grandchild sits still on the carpet between my knees, her back cushioned against the sofa, I consider detangling her springy hair coils. Hours earlier, I was settling into my babysitting routine as my daughter prepared for work. Between sips of morning coffee, I asked if she wanted me to fix her daughter's hair.

"No thanks, Mom," she replied. "It's healthier to leave it natural," snapping shut the lid to a plastic container holding her lunch. In an I-know-what's-best-for-my-child tone, she added, "I want her to have the mentality that her curl patterns are beautiful just by being free."

It is now late afternoon. Sunbeams peer through horizontal wooden blinds in the living room. One lands beside me, shining on the hair products I may use—shea butter and a bottle of coconut oil spray. How cute it would look to pass on to our little one a version of the girlhood hairdo my mother used to give me: side-by-side puffs and bangs.

In the 1940s when she was in her twenties, my mother, Laura Ann, would smooth her shoulder-length tresses into the peekaboo hairstyle of Veronica Lake, her screen idol. My mom and her girlfriends likely preferred a femme fatale look such as Miss Lake's for reasons they were unaware. Perhaps they were wanting to be more attractive to men, or unconsciously imitating white beauty standards. Or were they clueless hostages peeling away any layers of shame they held about their natural hair?

Black American women from the previous generation, in the early twentieth century, were sure to have had stories about or personally experienced enslavement. A quiet argument could ensue that rightly or wrongly, rejecting hairstyles like cornrows and plaits was a way to distance themselves from slavery. Despite any cultural norms or societal expectations to leave their versatile hair bushy, braided or hot-combed straight, my descendants' hair reflected what made them uniquely American.

By the 1950s, photos of my now-married mother depicted a hairstyle that hardly changed the rest of her life: a curly bouffant reminiscent of the vintage Barbie Doll Bubble Cut. Mom usually got her hair done at the Black-owned beauty salon on Chicago's South Side, 25 miles from our suburban home. A couple of times she did brave a nearby shop to get her gray roots dyed. But the white beauticians were unfamiliar with her hair type. She returned home with her wavy hair teased straight into a beehive style, sprayed to a stiff. The finished look resembled black-spun cotton candy. She washed it out the next day.

My girlhood hairstyles were controlled by my mother. I give her credit for earnestly trying to coif me and my younger sister's hair, but honestly, fixing it was not her strong suit. Instead of sending us off to our all-white Catholic school in neat ponytails, she added valuable minutes to harried school mornings by braiding our bristly hair the night before into one or two stubby, thick plaits. I slept with a nylon scarf tied around my head to hold it in place. Come morning, I firmly combed back any hair that may have come loose. But by lunchtime, the hair around my front and sides protruded like cat whiskers.

A special hair-fixing session would occur if Easter or school picture day was coming up. The routine would be set in motion before dinnertime. Shampoo hair, then untangle with a rinse-out cream conditioner. Mom took the plastic handle of a rattail comb and divided my dark brown hair into four sections and twisted it into loose buns. My hair dried while we ate.

After dishes were washed, Mom sat me in a kitchen chair. A terrycloth towel covered my shoulders. Following a stiff brushing, she poked the tip of the comb into my scalp and separated the hair into three sections: across the front for my bangs, and two parts down the middle. She slid long silver clips into the sections to keep them straight. Her two fingers scooped hair grease from the sky-blue glass jar of Posner Bergamot and oiled my scalp. The hot comb and curling iron, with their lingering burnt hair odor from earlier sittings, were heating up on the coil of the electric stove.

The pressing ordeal would begin. I squinched my eyes. She might start at my sides. So my forefinger held an ear down to protect the thin skin from being nicked with the metal teeth from the hot comb. When she took the iron to my "kitchen," the hair line at my neck and the hardest to get straight, I sucked in my breath. Still, nothing shielded me from the eventual prick of hot metal scorching my down-turned ear, singeing the front of my scalp or sizzling the nape of my neck. She would always apologize for her clumsiness. Her "I'm sorry," resembled what a stranger might say after accidentally bumping into someone: polite but said with fleeting sincerity. This was usually followed with a terse, "Sit still and stop being so tender-headed!" As if it was my fault she never learned how to use the irons.

Eventually, her efforts were complete. Where a chunky braid had once been was now a pair of curled-under ponytails held in place by coated rubber bands with clear plastic balls at either end. Atop my forehead sported a sausage bang, so named because of its obvious shape.

When I reached preadolescence in the late 1960s, Mom's lack of expertise in the kinky hair department prompted her to take me to Miss Michaels Beauty Salon, her hairdresser in the city. There, I would get my hair permed straight with a chemical relaxer.

There was a lot of social upheaval and intellectual shifting going on in America during this time, especially in 1968. The revered Dr. Martin Luther King, Jr. and Robert F. Kennedy would be assassinated. The Olympics in Mexico City saw two Black athletes stage a silent yet defiant act against racial discrimination in the United States. "Star Trek" aired television's first interracial kiss, despite a boycott threat from local TV affiliates in the Deep South. Anti-Vietnam War protesters made good on their promise to come to Chicago and disrupt the Democratic national convention.

In *Ebony* and *Jet* magazines, I had seen photos of Kathleen Cleaver, one of the prominent revolutionary women within the Black Panther Party. She was married to Eldridge Cleaver, the Minister of Information for the Panthers and came from a well-educated family. Her fair skin looked like she could be one of my peoples. Her dark hair, tapered at the sides, rose into voluminous, cylinder-shaped perfection. If only my hair could look like hers. I wondered how my schoolmates and the nuns would react (impressed or scared?) when I entered class bearing a symbol of the Black Power movement.

I recall spending a Saturday away from our suburban home at my father's drug store, a pharmacy he owned in Chicago. Per my mother's instructions, he gave me $15 to go to the beauty shop, located several streets away. It was time for me to get a touch-up since my relaxer had "grown out" an inch or two. Instead of catching a bus, I walked a block from my father's store to the neighborhood barber shop. I was 13 years old and decided me and my hair should appear more Afro-American (what we called ourselves back then).

The raucous banter of the barbers quieted when I entered. I became uncomfortable as they looked at me for some moments, then went back to the business of cutting hair and shaving faces. Their conversations, maybe about sports or politics, mingled with the R&B music coming from a portable clock radio on the counter. Most of them wore short-sleeved zip-up smocks. I felt self-conscious among the male customers sitting in a row of barber chairs covered in red Naugahyde.

With eyes fixed at my feet, I cleared my throat and directed a request to no one in particular. "Could someone cut my hair into an, um, natural?" My voice came out higher pitched than normal. A dashiki-clad barber must have felt my discomfort.

"Sweetheart, are you sure that's what you want?" A gold-capped front tooth glinted at me. I tried to look at his face and not his mouth.

"Uh-huh," I nodded. He gestured toward his empty chair and I took a seat. The backs of my thighs scratched against cracked fabric. Wish I'd worn long pants and not culottes, I thought.

With a slight whoosh, a white and blue-striped cotton sheet was draped over my blouse. "Goldie" snapped a metal button at the back of my neck. He had the fresh smell of Old Spice after-shave cologne, like my dad. The scissors went clip-clip. Facing the mirror, I watched my hair silently drift to the gray-tiled linoleum floor...

When my father saw where most of his $15 went, he made three disapproving "tsk" sounds with his tongue. Shaking his head back and forth, he said, "Wait until your mother sees what you did."

Sure enough, Mom did a double take when she saw my transformed shoulder length hair. It no longer looked like it belonged to a non-threatening member of the middle class, but to an aspiring, although awkward-looking Black Militant. My hair was now a lopsided three-inch high rectangle, shaped like a used pencil eraser. The short kinks on the back of my head were flattened out, probably from leaning against the car headrest on the ride back home. Or maybe it was cut wrong.

My mother struggled and asked me a string of questions. "What in the world did you do to your hair? Have you lost your damn mind?" She rarely cursed. I think she was embarrassed for me. Or thinking how I'd feel at Sunday mass the next morning when everyone would notice this abrupt change in my appearance. She tearfully reprimanded her husband for my disobedience, "I thought you sent her to Miss Michaels, not to a gotdang barber!"

When I got older and could pay for it myself, I got my

hair fixed in ways that appealed to me. It has had colorful beads attached to the tips of a hundred dangly micro-braids. I've had blonde extensions crocheted into my hair. Fingered into juicy curls. Wet set on spongey rods. Cornrows interlaced with gold thread. In a blue moon, I will (carefully) use the hot comb to touch up my edges. On a bad hair day, it gets covered up with a baseball cap or a head wrap. Before vacationing in Europe and Africa, a skilled braider gave me several long, thick plaits separated by zigzagging parts. I could enjoy my excursions, undistracted if humidity or some other element affected my hair. What a luxury.

Just as my mother took me to the beauty shop, I would do the same for my daughter.

When my Millennial was eight years old, I made morning appointments for us to get our hair done. At the shop, my daughter Jade could get a better hairdo than what I was capable of giving her (Yes, I inherited my mother's mediocre hair-fixing skills.). I wanted to look cute for a boyfriend's holiday work party that evening.

The beautician washed and pressed my daughter's hair, then sectioned it into a dozen squares and braided it. She secured Jade's hair in the familiar coated rubber bands, although these plastic balls were red, blue, and neon green. We left the salon and on the drive home, Jade blurted out, "I hate my hair like this."

I didn't feel the need to ask why she disliked the results. After all, I was the adult and paid good money to get her hair done.

"Don't be so dramatic. It's adorable," I said. "Think how easy it'll be to fix for school come Monday morning."

As a single mom, going on a fancy, or any kind of date,

was rare for me. My mother was giddier than me about my upcoming rendezvous. When we arrived at her condo for babysitting, she couldn't contain herself.

"He's such a nice young man. And he's a fireman?" she asked.

"Yes, Mom, but please don't make a big deal when he comes to pick me up, okay?"

"Well, let me get my camera so I can take a picture of you and Jade," she insisted. "You look gorgeous in that red dress, but," her eyebrows raised, "what kind of hairdo do you have?"

For 1993, I was quite on trend. The crown of my hair had been gelled into a crisp mound, rolled high into a sort of backward sausage bang. The rest of my medium length hair flowed into a soft flip.

My mother then regarded her granddaughter's hair. In her matter-of-fact way she said, "All those braids make her look like Medusa." Thank goodness Jade didn't know this was a reference to the Greek mythical creature, beautiful until Athena transformed her into a vicious monster with snakes for hair.

I clucked my tongue and let out one of those exasperated sighs that a daughter will give her mother when she says something ridiculous. "It does not," I said. "Please just take the picture already."

When I look at that Polaroid photo today, I still like my hairdo. But the forced smile on my little girl's mouth says, "I'm mortified."

As Jade got older, her self-confidence grew along with her ability to make her own hair decisions. However, the day she came home sporting a remarkably longer and fuller head of hair, the mom in me had to ask, "Is that a weave?"

"Why?" she asked.

"Cos I heard weaves could scar your scalp and make your hair fall out."

"Yeah, if it's a bad one," she added, "but mine is sewn-in. There are braids underneath that protect my natural hair. That'll make it grow faster."

"Maybe so, but your boyfriend," I joked, "is going to get his hand tangled up in all that fake hair when he tries to run his fingers through it."

In the long run, I was wrong. She was right. A good weave and proper care improved the health of her hair.

When Jade got married and became pregnant, her dense mane of hair prompted me to comment, "I hope you're not planning to keep in that weave while you're expecting. It might not be good for you."

"I haven't had a weave for months," she proudly informed me. "This is all mine," tossing back her fluffy mane to prove the point. "All these pregnancy hormones are making my hair grow."

Black hair beauty standards have evolved. Where some Black women in another time found it unsettling to see their hair in its natural state, Baby Boomers like me did not regard that as substandard. Today, the Millennials and Generation Z embrace a no-chemical look, spawning a thriving natural hair movement. Its broad influence finds more women and men of African descent keeping their natural afro-textured hair.

Will my grandchild's hair memories include a kitchen wafting of fried hair clinging to a hot comb? Probably not. In 10 or 15 years, will Beyoncé's daughters be the strong Black females whose hairdos she'll want to copy?

From my couch position in Jade's living room, I look

down at the tips of my granddaughter's corkscrew curls. They stand up like points on a princess's crown. Best to leave her hair in this naturally royal state. I dab some shea butter moisturizer, rub it between my palms and smooth it on her hair, delighted at her calmness to let me work it in. I reshape her coils. When a spray of coconut oil rests upon them like glittering pixie dust, I smile.

The moment will come when she appreciates hair as an expressive part of her identity. A physical connection to her African roots. Her hair, like that of the Black women before her, will remind the world of her place of origin, regardless of how she chooses to wear it.

Not from Around Here

Bill Stifler

As I was browsing the mythology section at McKay's Used Books in Chattanooga, Tennessee, a woman in her mid-thirties in the aisle with me looked up from where she was kneeling by the stacks and asked me, "Are you Jewish?"

"No," I said.

"Well, what are you, then?" she said.

"Pennsylvanian," I said.

I have lived in the Chattanooga area most of my life, thirty-seven years now, but I still think of home as Pennsylvania. For a long time, I thought I had lost my Dutch accent. Then about twenty years ago, a motorist with a flat tire pulled into my driveway in Ooltewah. I talked to him for a while, and he said, "You're from Pennsylvania, aren't you?" The accent was still there. Sometimes, I will hear a recording of myself on the phone, and the voice reminds me of my father's or one of my brothers'.

About fifteen years ago, I was in a laundromat in Cleveland, TN. Another patron was on his cell phone, and the longer he talked, the more I heard home in his voice.

After he finished his phone call, I asked him if he was from Pennsylvania. "No," he said, "Michigan."

"I thought I heard a bit of a Pennsylvania Dutch accent," I said.

"I did live in Glen Rock, PA, for several years," he said.

I explained that Glen Rock was just a few miles from where I had grown up.

In the South, people define themselves first and foremost as Southern. I suppose if asked to define ourselves regionally where I grew up, we'd say, Mid-Easterner or Mid-Atlantic, but the question would seem odd. Most of my neighbors were Pennsylvania Dutch, with names ending in -er. Stifler, Olewiler, Bortner, Frutinger, Dellinger, Stover, Kaltreider. And those whose names didn't end in -er mostly sounded German. Rexroth, Leiphart, Ludwig, Dagenhart, Parr. There were a few generic names, Taylor, Miller, and Robinson, but not many.

When the VW bug appeared in the '60's, the older people at church called it a "Wolksvagen," falling naturally into the German pronunciation. Even when I was a child, their voices always had an accent to my ear. And when old fashioned Sunday was celebrated at Windsor Church of God, a member of a Winebrennerian denomination split from the old German Brethren, the song service was in German, my mother, a Methodist from just over the border in Maryland, stumbling over some of the words and surprised at the fluency of my father, who seldom attended church, but had learned the songs as a boy with the Evangelical United Brethren. A few years ago, when my mother was visiting, someone asked her what our religious background was, and she answered, "Mennonite," which wasn't strictly accurate but was a clearer answer than many to my friends in the South who were largely unaware of the rich religious tradition inherited from the German states.

While I seldom eat pork and sauerkraut on New Year's, or feast on Lebanon bologna, or routinely use words like "nebby" or "doppy" or "fressen," at heart, I am still Pennsylvania Dutch. When I think of home, I think of the rolling hills of the piedmont along the Susquehanna River, of cornfields, tobacco fields, cow manure, and dairy farms, of apple orchards and well water, the cluck-cluck of pheasant in fall and the foggy breath of deer on a cold November morning.

Much of that world has disappeared in the years I have lived in the South. The pheasant are gone along with the tobacco fields and many of the farms. Clusters of condominiums sit where once were open pastures. The old Dutch farmers have been replaced by commuters from Baltimore and others who like the benefits of open country coupled with easy access to the major cities of the Mid-Atlantic.

But there are still those of us who remember. You will find us scattered around these United States, not from around here, sounding like home.

In Place

Elizabeth Templeman

It all began with Lyn. She was annoyed by the choice of theme for an upcoming conference.

This was a national conference on post-secondary teaching. Hosting it was a big deal for our small university. The theme was to be "intercultural diversity," meant to encompass diversity and acceptance in our teaching practices—surely a noble aspiration.

Lyn's point was that we're so focused on diversity, on *global* perspectives, on *internationalizing* our campuses, that we lose sight of the local: the distinct and distinguishing features of the ground beneath our feet. In a sense, we risk losing our sense of place, of where in the world we are at any given time. She showed up at my office, leaning against the door-jam, book-sack resting on her hip, exasperation lighting her eyes, maybe recognizing a shared inclination to contest the incontestable, to stir the waters now and again. We set out to draw others into what was promising to be a conversation with legs.

By the next week we were a group of four—ecologist, writer, geographer, and Canadian studies scholar—voices running over one another in a satisfying hour of discussion that flowed and diverged and converged. That national conference came and went; our group took hold, and grew. We invited a historian, a visual artist, a cultural geographer; later, an anthropologist. Even as the group grew to fold in others, it would take so little to refocus, and then to forge ahead, encompassing additional perspectives. We learned that we shared no common language for place; that we perceived and designated places in remarkably different ways.

A short walk to Guerin Creek, which carves its way, unnoticed, along the southern boundary of our campus, constituted one lesson in perspective. Guided by Tom, the geographer, we searched for traces of erosion, of water accommodating the lay of the land even as the community develops over and around it. I learned to notice silt and debris, but also absences of vegetation. Together, we read the story of the landscape, noticing hue and line, linking cause and effect. Above the creek bed, along the horizon, evidence of our expanding community asserted itself.

Our talks represent one of the joys of being an educator: the opportunity to think and act collectively, creatively, intellectually. This group is friendly, funny, and motivated by the promise of our what we might accomplish together. Even if we never accomplish anything tangible at all, for me the opportunity for our exchanges and for whatever subtle shifts in thinking we might provoke will have been enough.

You might well ask why it takes six scholars to debate the essential value of place. Or, indeed, wonder how convoluted our shared academic perspective has become that we accept as worthy of contention a notion that sense of place could be anything *but* central to our human sensibility. Yet it gets argued that the upcoming generation may have evolved intellectually and emotionally, to the extent that place may no longer be critical to identity, or family, or community, never mind to well-being. Holding in check both despair *and* cynicism had allowed me to relish the debate, and to renew—and to deepen—my own personal sense of location, and of local perspectives. As we've talked and read our way toward shared understandings, we've challenged each other to articulate assumptions, to question what, from within the safe confines of our disciplines, we had regarded as beyond question.

Consider, for example, the assumptions underlying how we even *name* a place. Our shared conventions will nudge us, without thought, to say that we work in Kamloops, this small city in the interior of BC. But how much richer with connotation, to know that I stand along the North Thompson watershed, on the sagebrush steppe within the Shuswap Highlands?

Finding our way toward a greater sense of place was, by turns, disorienting, and exhilarating. While the differences, discipline to discipline, surprised us, the emergence of common ground proved as unsettling. We came to realize that the shared pursuit of truth, a compulsion for more broadly recognized validity, may have propelled us, as academics within our siloed disciplines, to privilege abstraction over the specific. From a distance, that shift seems innocuous—incontestable, even. And yet, in that quest for the sweeping certainty, have we ceased to attend to the profusion of life beneath our feet? Swept away by our own generalizations, have we lost our mooring to place?

The challenge for our little group has been finding how, within the confines of those evolving conventions and abstractions, we might restore the value of the tangible; of the abundance of minute details that distinguish and imbue with meaning the spaces we walk upon and work and play within.

These currents of thought have, of course, spilled beyond the confines of my professional life. I can't overlook how I've been so drawn to this group, and these explorations, because I am, indisputably, a creature of place.

At the most personal level, place is the anchor: the rich soil in which we take root; the post by which we set our compasses. All of which are metaphors for stability. And yet, among my friends and family, I am most often the one oblivious to the markers of place. I know the inside of my home intimately, but only steps outside the door, the quality of knowing shifts to resemble an embracing cloud of familiar colour and texture and contours. I'm woefully ignorant about the names of grasses, flowers, and even trees—a fact made acutely evident by time spent with my ecologist friend. I mix up east and west, and am capable of not recognizing our own driveway on the rare occasion when a thick fog rolls along our road. I know discrete plots of ground—the beds in my garden, my running trails, our woodpile, the dog path—but connections between them, the broader context of place others around me seem to grasp so naturally, evade me.

The siren call of my inner thoughts—the flotsam of ideas and memories, the remnants of dreams—unhitch whatever receptors might have attuned my consciousness to position. Even along my familiar running trails I will awaken from reverie with no idea where I am along the path I'm running, or which way to turn when another intersects. This has happened twice in the past year and troubled me to the core each time. And yet, despite a dysfunctional register of place, I have a solid sense of being *at home* in a place. My husband would say (*does* say) that I'm a homebody—ridiculously set in my ways, captive to routine, smitten with tradition. (And surely place is the necessary ballast for ritual and routine.) He, on the other hand, has an acute sense of place and is astute in everything to do with orientation. He is also comfortable with travel, and with change; keen to explore *other* places. Two years ago, we began a running argument about spending Christmas in Hawaii (his idea). On a scale of one-to-preposterous, the idea strikes me as just this side of polygamy, or voodoo. We have Christmas here, at home. The turkey is in the freezer, after all. And then there's our annual walk on the lake before dinner ... the Boxing Day game at the rink ...

Maybe I should try to relax, allowing myself to drift more easily, freeing myself from that anchor, or tether. Maybe this generation has it right with their far-flung companions ever at their fingertips, able to sleep wherever they put down a sleeping bag. But I know that my own kids had to grow into that ease; that it didn't come naturally to them. When they were babies, our kids would never sleep away from home. We'd notice, with some envy, how other parent's toddlers would slump in easy sleep—in airports, on buses, on the couch of a friend after dinner. Not ours. They'd wrestle to stay awake, sometimes nodding into sleep just as we rounded the bend toward our driveway after hours of highway travel.

I remember as though it were yesterday, an amiable late-night dinner interrupted by the clattering of the wooden beads which separated bedroom from hallway in the ramshackle trailer of our still unattached, still ski-bumming, friend. This was the sign that our daughter, barely two and assumed to be asleep in the cozy nest we'd made of her own blankets, was indeed, not so. While we finished our meal, she staggered up and down the short hallway, cradling her beloved Baby and looking for all the world like a little drunk, cheerfully unsteady on her feet.

That child would love, for an interminably long time, a book about a kitten who wandered, lost, as one after another crudely rendered farm animals would ask, "Is *this* the place where you belong?" Our daughter, assuming the shrill, high-pitched voice she bestowed on that kitten, would call out the refrain: "No, No, *No!!* This is *not* the place where I belong."

If I had ever doubted that place matters, and how home is its essence, raising kids would surely have restored my certainty. In elementary school, each of them had routines of homecoming. Within seconds of the back-door slamming shut, backpacks would slump to the floor, and bathroom doors would bang. Home brought relief in the most visceral sense—even for the digestive track, it seems. Emerging from bathroom, they'd head for the fridge. Home seemed to arouse a thirst for milk. Even today, decades later, the soundtrack of their homecoming is a slamming back door, the thunderous dropping of shoes, the muted seal of fridge door, and a *thunk* of milk jug on counter.

I have my rituals of homecoming too. When I push through the door after a long day in town, an urge close to hunger is what I feel. I know it's more mental than physical—but give in to it, reaching for a cookie, cracker, or handful of dry cereal. Even before this, but less a matter of choice, twin habits of mine are to unclasp my watch and drop it in the outer pocket of my briefcase, and then to wash my hands. Only after the keeper of time is tucked away and the traces of outside are running down the drain do other cravings stir. And then I settle. A sure symptom of distress is to discover my watch missing from that pocket of my briefcase. Later, I find it in the oddest places—kitchen drawer, jacket pocket, front seat of car.

Every bit as predictable as my kids' routines—or my own—is the manner in which our homecoming is registered by our dogs. Since the kids were young, Miles, a border collie, had a unique routine to celebrate our returning home. However it may be that dogs conceive of place, they certainly demonstrate recognition of the momentous occasion of their humans returning to the home-place. While Blue, the heeler, patrolled the base of the driveway, Miles stopped at his bowl for a frantic few mouthfuls of food. Evenings, I'd extract myself and my stuff from the car to the sound of the aluminum dog dish pushed against gravel. The routine marking the return of the school bus was always more elaborate, because of its more predictable time perhaps, or because a kid's arrival is greater cause for celebration. Who can know? As Blue would dash down the driveway to meet the bus, Miles used to tear figure eights around the property: looping around the shop, down to the sheep pens, behind the barn, up past the woodshed, and back to the house.

All of our dogs live out their lives on the southernmost several acres of our property. To whatever extent that Miles and Blue were aware of place (or of life), their awareness must have derived from the multitude of changing smells, textures, movements and noises of our land. Included in that miasma would be their sense of us. Just as they registered our return home, so to, do they react to our wanderings. When we'd prepare for a trip, something—I suspect it's our preoccupation, or the packing of vehicles—tipped them off. Miles would stop eating and look what certainly could pass for depressed.

How could place be so ingrained in an infant's routine—indeed, seem so fundamental to even a dog's psyche—and yet cease to matter? How could we have become so sophisticated that the very notion of place becomes dispensable? It just doesn't figure. Among the articles our little group has shared is one by David Gruenewald. Drawing on other thinkers, Gruenewald argues for the distinction between the state of inhabiting a place and merely *residing* in one. Residence, he asserts, is a temporary state. When we reside in a place, we might invest little, and not surprisingly, also care little about that place. This brings to mind university dorm rooms (and accounts for, perhaps, the evolution of damage deposits).

To *inhabit* a place, on the other hand, implies the act of dwelling—of being at home; a far more elaborate and intimate relationship between creature and space. Fundamental to such a relationship is familiarity, and the attachment that extends from familiarity. If we appreciate the place we inhabit, we will tend to sustain it, and it, in turn, may be more capable of supporting us. That simple set of premises exposes what's at risk if we lose the capacity to know, deeply, the places we occupy in the world. It's a small step to the supposition that—if, indeed, this generation has ceased to know *how* to be attuned to place or lacks the capacity for attentiveness required for such knowing—we need to learn to teach those things.

If the generations following us don't know how to know their place, then, despite—or because of—the years of instantaneous exposure to information and entertainment, and whatever digital communities they invoke or embrace, surely they'll suffer from a state of placelessness, or rootlessness. If this is the trade-off for becoming internationalized, for residing in a global village, I can only worry for them, and mourn their loss. I do not believe for a moment that we, as humans—never mind as a particular generation—have sufficient capacity for knowing, heart for caring, or resources for investing, in place without bounds.

Human beings need home, however capable we may be of adapting to change, of picking up and creating a *new* home, or of tolerating a temporary one. If for nothing more than a point of reference for our poor extended brains— and maybe for our hearts too—we need to recognize where it is we are situated, and how to care about and to care for that place. We need names for its features, for its plants and creatures and landforms, just as we need its stories and the memories it has signified for others before us.

Being Home

Elaine Terranova

Optimism is in the air. Soldiers are coming back from the War and the baby boom is about to start. For the first time since the Depression, my father's diamond cutting business begins to thrive; so many engagements, so many diamond rings. Even at home Daddy is occasionally smiling. As for my mother, she can't take her eyes off a for-sale sign that has sprouted in a lawn across the way. And at last, my parents have their wish, private property, the American dream. At last, they can afford to own.

In the new house I have a room to myself. I could pick the paper on the walls and I did, pink with a repeating pattern of ladies in long skirts and big hats that I took for princesses. Footmen or messengers presented them with flower bouquets from admirers. There was even my own single maple bed, though everyone's socks and underwear was stored in my bureau drawers.

Like most row houses, the homes on our street rubbed shoulders so not much light got through, especially on one side. In front the sun angled in a little, but the glassed-in screen porch reflected it back. There are those who believe to this day that ours was the darkest house on the block. Did it seem to someone walking by unoccupied? Would anyone know we were there? Decades later, I meet two boys, now old men, who lived up the street. Neither remembers me, or any of my family. In fact, I begin to doubt us myself. When my old friend, Alvin, and I drive again through the neighborhood after an elementary school reunion and search for it, the house is no longer there. It has burnt down or vanished in some catastrophe, and only a bridge of grass remains between the two neighboring houses.

While we were living in it, ivy hugged the lawn and my mother bought and situated a park bench at the free side, the one closest to the front steps and not connected to the neighbor's lawn. My mother had a fondness for parks, those patches of green in a stone city. She convinced my father to walk miles sometimes, not easy with his limp, so we could all go sit in Burholme Park. It became a Sunday ritual, maybe a reminder of the promenades of gentlefolk she had witnessed in Europe in her childhood. To my mother, her lawn was an annex of the park. Seated on the bench she felt she was not at home but in a garden, someplace she had purposely come.

When I return as a grown woman, the walls seem to have slid forward, the whole place smaller than I remember. The narrow hall from the kitchen to the dining room is a bottleneck, a little like the birth canal, I felt, because it was where I'd leave my mother and breakfast finished, pass the open door to the cellar steps where anything could be waiting, go out into the rest of the house, the rest of the world, school, for instance, or wherever I had to be.

But today I'm going the other way. I find my mother still in the dark blue dress, the color of her wedding dress, worn to sit *shiva,* the period of mourning for a loved one, even though the black cloths that draped the mirrors are gone. Her lips have the thin veneer of lipstick almost worn off. It was meant for special occasions only, and she applied it in two dabs smeared with her little finger to even it out.

The kitchen seems aglow as I pass through the dim screen porch, the French doors to the living room, the open, vanished partition leading to the barely used dining room. Then that narrow passage to the kitchen where Mom sits on one of the white, painted chairs pulled up to the red and white checked oil-cloth of the table. When I first went to school, after what felt like a lifetime of waiting, she became Mom, no longer Mommy. I never said Dad, though—even now when he is gone, he is still Daddy.

If my mother is waiting for him to return, as she used to, the day will never end for her. She won't know what to do.

"What will I do?" she asks. There is no precedent for going on without him, even for eating or preparing a meal for herself. This house, the scene of so many battles and misunderstandings between you two. Where you were drummed out of the religion by her and the rabbi's wife, though you never gave it up. Where your wedding to someone of a different faith meant the end of your welcome here.

"I know what you must feel. I do. I have a husband now. I can't imagine what it would be to lose him." Will she say something wounding in response? It's what I expect, still raw from the recent past. But "You're just kids," she says. "You're just married. I lived with your father 40 years."

In a shopping bag I carry veal from the nearest kosher butcher. There's a frozen vegetable in the fridge. I have never been encouraged to cook in this kitchen but now she will not put up a fight. Back from Rome where we have gone to live, I am heady with European cuisine, I've read Julia Child and gone to restaurants. Tonight, I will try to make veal scallopini. But the only wine to be found in the house is in the pantry, reserved for Passover. Gamely, I open the jug of Manischewitz and cook with it and pour a little for both of us to drink.

I have put my battered suitcase, my father's varnished straw suitcase which he took once to Europe on a diamond-buying trip, upstairs on the bed of my childhood room. How narrow and monastic it feels, the single bed I was so happy to have at six, when the family moved here, and I no longer had to sleep with my mother.

My brother Sidney would like me to stay forever, isn't it a daughter's duty? To leave my husband and move back to take care of our mother. She is so vulnerable and receptive, so unthreatening at this moment. I will stay, but not forever.

The next morning, I walk downstairs into the too quiet, too empty first floor and feel my father's presence. The living-room chair where he sat a little separate from the rest of us, the green mohair armchair under the lamp, to read The Bulletin after work. So rare when he looked up to smile, to speak, I couldn't remember if he actually had or if it was something I'd only wished for. But how important just his presence, how glad I was we could count on it, even if everyone knew to leave him alone after the exhaustions of the day.

I look up the polished hardwood stairs where he once caught me when I stumbled down from the second floor.

"Dolly!" he cried. He came as fast as he could and cradled my head in his arms, closer maybe than we'd ever been. And in a loving, gentle voice as he held me, crooned, "Dolly, are you all right? You're all right?" So I saw him, on the stairs too, kneeling over me. And at the kitchen table, in a desperate hunger that must have haunted him from his impoverished childhood, stuffing in mouthfuls he scarcely looked at.

In the years they lived alone together, after the rest of us were gone, did my mother stand over him, serving, or join him with her plate at the side of the table? I can see them sitting together, talking quietly (could they?) as they ate. I hoped that was how it was. And imagined them, evenings, watching the TV in silence, keeping each other company. I knew there were middle of the night calls to the hospital when the paramedics came, another heart attack or the fear of one. But easy sleep too, maybe, other nights. Or did they stay up arguing, gnashing over my father's concerns, as they had all those nights I couldn't sleep, hearing them from my bed in the middle room? And were the enemies that had mocked and threatened him all now locked within his body and taking the shape of illnesses?

For a while after he retired, my father had fitted up a workbench and a wheel to cut diamonds at home. He would, of course, want to help out my brother Leo, who had taken over the shop downtown. A space was swept and cleared out in the dark jumble of the cellar and a standing lamp brought down. I could see him, smiling to himself, the jeweler's loupe to his eye, dimples in his cheeks like my brother Sidney's. Maybe Leo didn't need him but Daddy would want to believe he did, that he could still keep his hand in, be useful.

There was a tender pride he took in me too at the end of his life which was new. Instead of discouraging my ambition to be a writer—as he had when I was in school, "Only one in a million makes it"—he hoped I'd put my maiden name, his name, on the masthead of the union newspaper I edited. But it was too late; I'd already started with my married name. Oh, I wished I'd changed it just to please him.

Unthinkable, that I would never now be able to sit with him, his arm thrown over my shoulder, as I'd wished for and imagined a million times.

Before the kitchen, of course, lies the dining room. Odd designation because it was so rarely used for dining, only on holidays or the two times my brothers invite the women they will marry to our house to meet the family. Not true, sometimes even after the marriages, on occasional Friday nights for Sabbath dinner. Leo's wife will hate these evenings, the same plain food, a stuffed capon, oven-roasted potatoes, an overdone vegetable, but fresh, not canned, my mother would say in pride. Bobbi will be dressed up with earrings and perfume for their date afterward, a movie or a party. For reserved, red-haired Selma, in awe of Sidney's mother, this dinner is an evening out. I appreciate the variety and company, my mother's efforts at preparation despite her advanced years when most dinners are leftover based. I try to be at home those evenings, glad the room and the house don't recede into their usual darkness.

If we'd had something like an altar to household gods, it would be positioned here in the dining room. It's an odd room with a conglomeration of furniture, Louis XIV to Scandinavian modern, and other eras in between. The large wooden dining table, ladder chairs with crisscrossed panels are pulled under it, that my mother stood before to light Sabbath candles on Friday nights. The same table I did stunts and roller skated on when I was little. Lining the walls are a china closet, a buffet, and a bureau with a mirror above it, remnants of previous households, my family's or second-hand purchases from a neighbor who was moving. An embroidered scarf is spread over the bureau and what surprises and touches me, it's topped with my framed high school graduation picture. I think of my mother's face behind me once in the mirror watching me comb my hair. Out of nowhere she said, wistfully, fondly, "You have a noble forehead, like your father."

And I remember her fresh from the shower, hair just washed in Emulsified Coconut Oil Shampoo. The sweet smell that moves with her, even after she ties her toweled hair in a flowered silk kerchief. It wafts with her down the stairs to the dining room where she has already laid out silver candlesticks on one side of the white, lace-edged tablecloth in preparation. She takes up a book of matches that came with Sidney's cigarettes and strikes one that she sets to the wicks of the Sabbath candles. There is no other light in the dusky room. Then she closes her eyes, praying, and waves her arms in wide arcs. The shadows of her movements beat against the walls like wings of a great, dark bird.

Articles of faith were stored in the top drawer of the mirrored bureau, red and blue velvet drawstring pouches where the *twillim* were kept that my brothers wrapped around their arms to say daily morning prayers, nodding their heads forward and back, and my father did, too, once in a while. They could have seen themselves in the mirror above as they *davened* but didn't look. I have a flash in my mind even now of one of them with the square leather phylactery on his forehead, looking like an Egyptian god. Also kept here, yarmulkes and prayer books in Hebrew I couldn't read. That's where the holiness ended. Embossed tablecloths and napkins and fill-in linens from the dime store were laid in the drawers below.

It's late afternoon. I've been with my mother almost a week now. The dining room is partially lit by a thread of sun from the one window at the side and rear where my family's house divided from the neighbor's. My mother comes out from the kitchen which is and always has been her habitual lair and into the dining room to sit with me, as if I were a guest. She's remembered I don't belong here.

"What will you do with his things?" I ask. I'm thinking I could help her pack them up.

"Sidney is coming for the shirts and jackets and his bathrobe. Not the underwear."

"What for?"

She raises her eyebrows, looks at me like I'm an idiot. "He'll wear them. But not the underwear. It's too big."

At first I think this is in the interest of thrift, maybe a little creepy. But then I understand. He wants to put on clothes my father wore, as if to find something of him still inside.

And when my mother leaves the room, when she in fact goes up the stairs for the bathroom or to rest, I'm drawn to the hall closet where my father's overcoat and hats were kept, and the cardigan he wore around the house. I feel like a trespasser, it's not my house any longer, hasn't been for years, but some force draws me to the pearl knob, and, after a moment's hesitation, I turn it and pull the door open. The two hats share the upper shelf, just as he'd left them. Wearing a hat inside the house was bad luck, a superstition of my mother's. But my father wore one to *daven* in, it was what old men did even in synagogue. I reach for the worn felt brim of the closer, grey one and take it down. My fingers circle the indentation, the crease my father pinched into the crown every time he wore it. The felt is soft and cool. I could be holding my hand over his hand as it makes the familiar motion.

And then I look around, lost suddenly. Without him, could this house ever really be home to me again?

On a Rocky Inland Coast

Lee Zacharias

I came to Greensboro from the Ozark Mountains in Arkansas and to Arkansas from the Blue Ridge Mountains of Virginia. For a couple of years before that I lived in Richmond, with its then thriving downtown and the tumbling rapids of the James River, in a funky urban neighborhood called the Fan, the ocean a short two-hour drive away, mountains even closer. And before that? Let's just say that for the twenty-five years that led up to my move south, I was a Midwesterner longing to escape the bland flatlands and ranch houses of my youth.

I arrived in Greensboro, never having seen it, in August of 1975. That past winter I had accepted a teaching job at the University of North Carolina Greensboro over the phone, the only job I could get without a campus interview. UNCG had interviewed me in December, at the Modern Language Association conference in New York, where the professor sent to entertain me while I waited in the hotel hall told me how much I would like Greensboro because there were no bars, everyone went to church, the neighborhoods were all new, and it was a great place to raise a family. At the time I was in the middle of a divorce. I had no children, and every virtue he named seemed a demerit to me. The interview went no better. The department head never looked up as he read course descriptions from the college catalogue and asked how many could I teach? I thought I'd rather crawl into a coffin, but then a bad flu turned into pneumonia on a bone-chilling rainy January night in New Orleans, where I had gone for my first on-site interview, and I was out for the season. I didn't choose Greensboro; it chose me.

And so that August I set out with a carsick puppy beside me on the front seat of a twenty-four-foot U-Haul and all my worldly goods rattling around the back because the ten-foot truck I'd reserved had transmission problems and the bigger truck was the best the office could do. It was evening by the time I backed it down my mountain driveway and into a ditch, night by the time I reached I-40, where I discovered that all the motels from Fort Smith to North Carolina were full. I spent my one overnight on the road trying to doze on the front seat with my head in a pool of puppy vomit at a truck stop outside of Little Rock and rolled into Greensboro near midnight the next day, wanting nothing more than a shower and a beer. I drove for miles before I found an open convenience store. It was 12:05 on a Saturday night (or Sunday morning, depending on how you mark time), and there was a big sign on the cooler that said NO ALCOHOL SALES AFTER MIDNIGHT. Arkansas had no Sunday sales either, but we were near the Oklahoma border, and on CDT back in Fayetteville there were fifty-five minutes left before the drive-thru window of the package store went dark.

The 7-Eleven was the second disappointment of the

night, because I had hoped that Greensboro might be in the mountains, in the foothills at least. It was dark by the time I passed Asheville and braked my way down Black Mountain, but I could feel the land unroll beneath me. Indeed, when I woke the next morning, I was in the flatlands again, and before anyone objects let me say that while Greensboro appears hilly to those who arrive from the coast, it most decidedly does not to anyone driving in from the mountains. I looked for a river. The downtown was in its last stages of decay and the ocean a long two hundred miles away. My Renault, which had been driven by a friend (who was supposed to drive the truck, but that's another story), had broken down on the trip and needed parts that never seemed to come. Students had claimed all the rental property near the university, and the one place I toured that would allow pets was a cramped duplex overlooking the city's water treatment plant. I spent most of my first semester commuting the six miles to campus from an apartment near Guilford College on a bus that had only one scheduled run in the morning and another in the afternoon, and though logic tells me it can't possibly have rained every day, the details of memory are stubborn. What I recall is waiting for the inevitably late bus in a downpour that lasted three months.

"It's just a year," my boyfriend and I assured each other when he arrived. "A year and we're out of here." We missed the built-in community of grad school, where we had met. He commuted to adjunct teaching at Elon College a few towns away, and out in the suburban land of no sidewalks, no friends, and not one street that could be crossed safely on foot, both of us felt stranded. We were writers, we'd come up through the '60s, we were rebels, for God's sake, and after the rough edge of the Ozarks Greensboro seemed overly civilized. We didn't even know where to buy pot.

Yet here we are decades later. What we found was a community of talented, accomplished, and unpretentious writers, quite unlike the posturing, competitive writing environment we had come from. My then boyfriend, now my husband of more than thirty years, taught another year at Elon, then for fourteen at Bennett College, one of two HBCUs in Greensboro, before moving on to finish his career at High Point University. Even before he retired, he found another calling in Hospice, and for the past many years he has been a volunteer for one of the best chapters in the nation. Midway through our second year we bought a little house in Latham Park, and on its screened porch I finished my first novel, which paid for the big old barn where we still live in Sunset Hills. In it we raised a son, we are part of a neighborhood that is hardly new, our dog patrols its sidewalks, we have friends throughout the city. The downtown underwent a renaissance and is now thriving. And I found my way to Ocracoke. Its wildness, its marshes, forests, and long stretch of untamed beach are my church.

But each time I returned from the island, as we sat on our back deck gazing out over the azaleas, I would say, "Well, it's not Ocracoke, but it's not bad." No matter how welcoming, there's not much a city can do to change its location, to build a mountain range or import a shoreline.

Until the storm.

My husband was en route to visit a friend in Detroit the day our landscape changed. I had been doing yard work— by then I had lovely flower garden along the back fence in addition to the vegetable patch behind the garage—and was standing on the side deck chatting with my next-door neighbor when I saw a roiling wall of black approaching from the west. At the same moment my son looked out the window of his English classroom at Grimsley High School. "Holy shit!" he said and was promptly sent to detention as the teacher slammed the shade down and attempted to go on with the lesson. What I said was "I'd better close the garage door," though by the time I reached it I was running. I made it back to the deck and was just though the door when glass began to shatter, the wind tore off gutters along with part of our roof, and trees began to topple. The largest of several we lost was a maple in the center of the backyard that split in three directions. "Holy shit," my son said again when he came home at lunch and opened the gate to find me in a backyard full of downed hardwood. I phoned ahead to my husband's friend and said, "Tell him to call home as soon as he gets there. We've had a tornado." It was not, according to the meteorologists, who called it a microburst, even a gustnado, but as I say memory is stubborn.

The stump that was left when trees surgeons cleaned up the mess was ninety-three inches across. Because the stump grinders were backlogged, I had an entire summer to contemplate the hole it would leave behind. I didn't know that the stump grinder leaves a mini-mountain rather than a hole, but this was at the height of the water-garden craze, and I figured that if I could not live beside a mountain stream or at the ocean, I would build my own right in my backyard.

The grinders left their hill, but I was unfazed. I hired two teenagers to dig. They were school dropouts, later heroin addicts, who wore tee shirts advertising their band,

Pugnacious Bastards, and whose every other word to me was "please" or "thank you." These were boys who never bathed, and whenever one entered the house it was an effort not to gag, but I've never hired better or more honest workers. The yard was nearly impossible to dig, given the massive tree roots spread beneath the baked brick of heavy clay soil, but the Pugnacious Bastards persisted. Where roots as dense as petrified wood protruded into the growing hole they terraced shelves for plants. Of my flower garden these two beautiful, unwashed boys who would go on to such rough times said, "It's so pretty. Would you mind if we just sat here for a minute?" Every break they took they insisted upon deducting from their wages, and I winced at the inked thumbprints on the canceled checks, because what those prints said was that they had no bank accounts, no home in the civilized world, they were institutionally suspect. As for the pond, they got so carried away that the center is over waist deep and I had to order a custom liner because the largest one available would not fit.

I bought a ton of rocks to line its shore, another to build a waterfall. Over the years I've added at least two more tons, some stones I've purchased, some given by the friend who later killed himself, some I've picked up on my travels. There are lava rocks from Costa Rica, cobbles from the Côte d'Azur, small boulders from the Tennessee River, pebbles worn smooth by the waves of Lake Michigan and Lake Superior up in Michigan's north woods, others I no longer remember pocketing. I added plants, including a yellow iris that has spread throughout the yard, two water lilies, and the underwater oxygenators recommended by the books. My bright koi, fantails, and shubunkins felt so at home that I fed them only once before they recognized my footstep and swam to the side, thrusting their mouths up out of the water to nibble from my hand. Dragonflies rested on the reeds. Wasps dipped their heads from their narrow waists to drink. In winter from the second-story window of my study I watched crows skate across the ice, buoyed by the happy babble of their caws. In the summer my mother loved sitting on a bench to observe the robins, the cardinals, the titmice, and sparrows come to bathe and splash. Our older son, my stepson, and I spent hours of his visits on that same bench, seeking Ghost Fish, a small, elusive second-generation gray shadow darting beneath the lilies. Nature frolicked.

Nature exploded.

What you learn when you attend its church is that the serpent does not invade the garden. The serpent *is* the garden.

The fantails were the first to die, followed by Roy the Koi, named by our younger son, but the shubunkins were so hardy they soon became enormous. They were also prolific breeders, so well fed they had no need to eat their own fry. I started with eleven fish and soon had a bio-overload of more than two hundred. I cut off the food supply and let nature take its course. Even so filtration was a problem. Every other week I had to crawl under a thorny rambler rose to unplug and move half a ton of rocks to expose the heavy, drum-shaped above-ground filter, drag it over to the grass and hose it down, move more rocks to pull out the clogged pump and jet-spray the muck. The accordion material inside the filter swelled, and it became harder and harder to reassemble and seal. I bought the expensive UV sterilizer recommended by the experts, which required a second pump to clean, but still the water clouded, and when the weather warmed the next spring I was out there swirling a toilet brush, trying in vain to collect the veils of bright green algae. I built a bio-filter that worked like magic, overnight the water so clear you could toss in a penny and make out the words "In God We Trust," until one day early the next spring, that is, when I stepped into the backyard to find my fish struggling to swim at the bottom of a mud hole. The bio-filter, the whiskey-barrel-sized rubber tub I had filled with pebbles and plants and buried beneath the waterfall—a waterfall I've rebuilt, rock by rock, well over a dozen times—was bulging with the expanding roots of the plants, and the water from my pond was leaking over the back and sides. I took it apart, rinsed batch after batch of pebbles in a kitchen colander and put it back together again, this time with a single plant, but even that one plant grew such vigorous roots that the first warm day of the next spring my pond drained itself again. I gave up on the bio-filter and found a packet of crystals billed as a natural water clarifier. It too worked like magic, and for easy refills I anchored the plastic dispenser beneath a flagstone with six-pound test line, though of course the line broke and the dispenser disappeared. After that I just threw the packets in, which worked fine until Lowe's stopped stocking them. For a year or two I bought them online, but then the retail source disappeared from the web, though I could still get them if I really wanted—all I would have to do is open a dealership.

These days when I spy a great blue heron crossing our yard as I sit upstairs writing I no longer reach for my camera but beat on the window, shouting, "You leave my fish alone!" Neighborhood cats did away with the fish in the small other pond I installed early on to serve as an isolation ward for one who seemed sick but turned out to be pregnant, but even though that pond has long since been filled in and the big pond is deep enough for the remaining fish to elude them, the cats love to scamper about the edges, chasing birds, overturning potted plants, knocking rocks and statuary in.

The two lilies that turned out to be a waxy white instead of the promised deep pink overgrew by the second year and began climbing the rocks like kudzu, their roots so stubbornly wrapped around the stones on the bottom I had to hire a man to pry them out and start over with a new one, though even a single lily will overgrow the second year, I've discovered, and I am perpetually in the market for muscle. Except for the iris, most of the marginal plants died the first winter, but the oxygenators proved so invasive that at times my little paradise looked more like an overdressed salad than a pond. It took me years to rid myself of them.

Have I mentioned the magnolia tree with its steady rain of leathery leaves and pods? Or the wisteria, the wild grapevine, and clematis that come up through the rocks to climb the nandina forest I planted behind? The morning glories brought by birds? This year I dug up the nandinas, so that I can at least spot the vines and spray when they sprout, a technique that does not work in the bed of day lilies I planted to mimic the pond's curve.

In short I discovered that maintaining a pond in one's backyard is about as much trouble as maintaining a vacation home in the mountains or at the coast.

But there it is, a little heaven that contains its own hell but is much too big for me to take out. These days my husband and I rarely sit out to share a drink before dinner. When we do he complains of the bugs, and while the fish take care of the mosquito larvae and the yard is no buggier than anyone else's, the dog won't rest until he coaxes someone to play ball. Instead we watch the news or take pause on the screened porch. Even so the pond offers both of us moments of respite as deep as its reflections, the crabapple blossoms in early spring, the moon late at night, even the sharp white pitch of the garage roof against a gloss of blue sky. The most ordinary things are made miracles inside its mirrored pool, and to watch the fish swimming about is as calming and restorative as the practice of yoga. There is a history piled in its rocks and sunk below its surface, those weeks of grace given to those boys who dug it and then came back to sit beside it when it was filled, the dragonflies, the birds, the wasps, the family members, some gone, others distant, the friend we still miss who brought us the rocks from the Tennessee River; a present and a future in the delight of a neighbor's grandchild as she scatters food for those otherwise self-sufficient fish. And in the trickle of water over stone each time I return from the mountains or the coast I hear its message: *listen,* it whispers, *you are home.*

Triumph

Madelaine Zadik

The Holocaust is my home.

As I look at these words, I am shocked. Millions of people would have been very happy if they only could have left home and left the Holocaust behind. So, how is it that I can claim the Holocaust as home?

I went to see the play, *The Last Rat of Thereisinstadt*, which explores life in the "Ghetto Town" of Terezín, a concentration camp that was located in Czechoslovakia. The Nazis used this place as a model camp, a showcase to provide proof to the world that they were taking good care of the Jews and were giving them a nice home. The inhabitants certainly didn't think of it as home, however. After the performance, during a discussion with the audience about what constitutes home, one of the puppeteers for the play said that, rather than a specific place, art was her home. As I was contemplating this concept, I suddenly had the revelation about the Holocaust comprising home for me.

What does home actually mean? Is it a place, a habitat, somewhere that provides shelter and safety, or is it a country, a community, or a state of mind? Is it the place where you feel most comfortable? What is it that makes one feel "at home?" The dictionary defines home as a house, apartment, or other shelter that is the usual residence of a person or family, or the place in which one's domestic affections are centered.

The Holocaust has always been a dominating force in my life. It was the world of my childhood. My parents and almost all the adults in their circle of friends were Holocaust survivors. The neighborhood where I grew up in northern Manhattan on the border of Washington Heights and Inwood was sometimes referred to as the *Fourth Reich* or, more kindly, *Frankfurt on the Hudson*, because of the high concentration of German Jewish refugees. Many of the shops along Nagle Avenue and Dyckman Streets could have just as easily been in Berlin or Hamburg. There was the Alpine Bakery, where one of the women behind the counter had a visible tattooed number on the inside of her forearm. That bakery is where we got rye bread with caraway seeds and *korn* bread, my father's favorite. There was no corn in it. *Korn* in German means grain. It was a dense whole grain bread. I've never had anything quite like it since, but to this day I prefer dense bread. No wonder bread for me.

My mother purchased imported cheeses from a woman named Suzy who had chubby pink cheeks and knew my mother by name. She also sold various types of pickled herring, which were displayed in glass vats in a refrigerated case. Just a few stores down the street was a deli, where pickles floated in big barrels filled with brine, and you could get one for a nickel. Although there was a small supermarket, everyone used the specialty stores for most of their shopping. They got meat at the butcher shop.

Fish and vegetables were procured at small niche markets. There was one store that sold only imported goods, mostly European to appeal to the tastes of the neighborhood clientele. That is where my mother would get her stash of German marzipan. American marzipan would not do!

On Sunday afternoons, families gathered for *Kaffe und Kuchen* at Nasch Bakery on Dyckman Street, which served full meals as well as sweets. The mural on the wall created an ambiance of a European café. I loved the custard filled Napoleons. Sunday was also the day for strolls in Fort Tryon Park, especially around the Heather Garden overlooking the Hudson River and the cliffs of the New Jersey Palisades on the other side. It was a horticultural paradise in the midst of the city. The benches along the main promenade were occupied by families and friends discussing the news of the day, while young children ran around. The air was filled with the sound of German and a variety of fragrances emanating from the neatly maintained flowerbeds. I remember my mother swooning when the linden trees were blooming. That was a sense memory of her childhood home.

My parents and their friends mostly spoke German to one another, and my parents proudly had me display my German skills whenever friends were visiting. I always hated the public presentation that was required of me. When their friends would remark how cute I was, I began refusing to perform.

One of parents' friends became a professor at the City College of New York and counseled young men on how to evade the draft. He had gone to George Washington High School with Henry Kissinger and remembered how classmates had labeled Kissinger as the least likely to succeed.

On Nagle Avenue, just up the block from my elementary school, PS152, was the neighborhood YM&YWHA. I went there as a kid, but they also had programs for adults. My father had a regular card group that met to play a German game called *Skat*. Even after my parents moved out of the neighborhood to Riverdale in the Bronx (while I was away at college), my father would go back to the Y for that card game and also to volunteer in their senior lunch program. Dr. Ruth Westheimer (aka Dr. Ruth), also a resident of Washington Heights, was on the board of the Y and is still on it to this day. In fact, she still lives in that neighborhood.

I didn't know all my parents' friends' histories, but I knew they had left the country of their birth not by choice, and that they were the lucky ones. They had managed to hide, to escape, to survive and to start life anew. They had thought they were at home in Germany, but that idea was turned on its head.

As a child, I experienced the Holocaust as a fixture of our household—always there in the background, immovable. My aunt Helga's absence was a part of the carpet and the air, as was the absence of all those other people pictured in the photo albums that my mother had so carefully carried with her to China, then across the Pacific Ocean, and cross country to New York City. That included *Tante* (aunt) Klara; uncle Benno; and my father's parents. Others in the pictures were now living in France, or Israel, or Australia. Some of my parents' friends were from their eight years living in Shanghai, the only place that in 1939 would take in Jewish refugees with no money and without a visa. My parents were among over 20,000 Jews who found refuge in Shanghai and formed a community in exile, but it was not a permanent home. The United States finally allowed them into this country in 1947. They had official papers saying they were stateless—another kind of homeless. Once in New York, they made new friends, some of whom had survived the Holocaust in the Philippines or watched parents being murdered while they hid in haystacks. Even as this refurbished life was molding itself around a new narrative in the United States, the Holocaust remained as part of the scenery. The old stories, the accented English, the pain of what was lost, and the scars, both physical and psychic, could not be expunged from the scene. As I was growing up, my life was wallpapered with these unerasable details.

My sense of home, the familiar, is what I feel when I hear someone speaking German. No matter where I am, I am drawn to the voices. It is the sound of home. It was a shock when at some point I learned that not all Germans were Jewish! It wasn't until I was a teenager that I even realized that my parents spoke English with an accent. In fact, I first learned that refugee English from my parents, as evidenced on a recording made when I was five years old. I lost my accent when I started going to school but not my affinity for the German language. Other Jews, and especially those from families that were not of German origin, cannot understand my fondness for German. To them it is the language of the oppressor. When they hear it, it definitely does not make them feel at home.

I grew up eating German foods: *Rollmops, Brathering, Mohnkuchen, Milchreis,* and *Rotkraut.* More than food or language, however, it is the sorrow that is so familiar—my mother's grief over having lost her sister Helga. My mother did not dwell on it, but subconsciously, that pain was infused into every meal that we were having but Helga was not. It made me very sensitive to the suffering in the world, to the horrors of war, and the plight of other refugees. I carried that on my shoulders as if I were Atlas. It didn't feel like a burden. It was just my life. This is how things were. Home was a place filled with grief, loss, and pain.

Yet, I didn't experience the Holocaust. I wasn't there. It is not my story. I lived through the aftermath, the rebirth after the horror. My mother was an incredible survivor. She knew she was lucky to be alive, and that was not to be taken for granted. I experienced her ability to find tremendous joy every day, her capacity to fill me with love, and to live life to the fullest. On weekends we went on excursions out into the country. Bear Mountain State Park, about an hour's drive north along the Hudson River, was a favorite. My mother always packed scrumptious picnic lunches for us, everything homemade, gourmet even by today's standards. Jones Beach was another favorite destination. In addition to hiking my mother loved swimming. She was quite the athlete. She even learned how to waterski well into her 40s. I have pictures of her doing headstands on the beach. She also went skiing in Fort Tryon Park, just across the street from our apartment building along Broadway. That park became a favorite hangout for me and my friends. I made myself at home high up in my favorite weeping willow tree and in the secret caves along the path on the side of what we called Devil's Hill. My mother was determined that Hitler would not win by robbing us of the enjoyment of all that life offers. No opportunity was to be wasted. That imperative was a lesson I learned at home.

My home now is filled with shelves of books about the Holocaust, including many first-person accounts, books about the next generation, children of survivors. I also inherited my mother's collection on the topic. I have a framed woodcut of Wroclaw that my mother bought on our postwar visit to Poland in 1967. It had been the city of Breslau, Germany, when my parents were growing up, the third largest Jewish Community in Germany. When we went back to that city, it clearly wasn't home anymore. No one speaks German. Everything is Polish. My mother's apartment building was no longer standing, and many other landmarks my mother searched for had disappeared. The synagogue where my parents were married had been desecrated and was totally dilapidated, with a dirt floor and paint peeling off the walls. The whole city still had a bombed-out look to it at that time, with much rubble lying around. The city my parents knew had vanished, but they showed little emotion. I remember being surprised by how stoic they were when I was feeling bombarded by sadness. I guess they survived it all by compartmentalizing and keeping those emotions at a safe distance. My mother had such wonderful memories of her childhood home. Perhaps she didn't want to destroy those as well. We also visited friends in Germany. My mother was interested in showing those places to me, but she was very clear that she never wanted to live there again. She had a new home.

In the 1980s, I joined a group of Jewish Lesbian Daughters of Holocaust survivors. Here I found another home. We understood each other in ways no one else could. Our experiences required no explanation. We held retreats twice a year. We explored our identities. We told our stories and our parents' stories. We shared the oddities of our childhoods. One woman talked about how as a kid she had a Barbie doll and a Hasbro easy bake oven. She recalled that she used to play *Barbie goes to Auschwitz*.

While we were all shocked, we weren't surprised. The Holocaust had become embedded in us.

It is now 75 years since the Holocaust. My parents are no longer alive. I no longer wish to live in this Holocaust home. However, I don't quite know how to get away from it. How do I find another home for myself? It raises a lot of questions about identity. Without it, who am I?

The truth is, I have made a new home for myself, a life far away from the urban streets where I played hopscotch. I live in rural western Massachusetts. There are forests and streams. People go cross-country skiing and hiking in the woods. On recent trips to Germany, I visited the countryside and realized that I now live in the landscape of my parents' youth. They had filled me with stories of their idyllic childhoods. My mother talked about the nature youth group with whom she went on camping trips, how she loved jumping from stone to stone as they crossed streams, and how they skied from town to town, taking the train back. No wonder my parents loved visiting me and felt so at home here.

I identify as a child of Holocaust survivors, however that is not the sum total of my being. My background and what my parents experienced has informed my life and made me who I am, but it doesn't have to confine me. Although I will always carry my first home with me, I don't have to live there permanently anymore. I can visit, but also take my leave. My parents escaped to freedom and were successful in creating a better life for themselves and for me. They would not want me stuck in that old home. They would be thrilled to know that today I can be at home in many different places. Coming from such a horrific legacy, that is the real triumph.

Contributor Biographies

Johnnie Bernhard is a traditionally published author of Upmarket Fiction. Her latest novel, *Sisters of the Undertow* was released in February 2020. Her novels are available in bookstores and online.

Rick Campbell lives on Alligator Point, Florida and writes poems and essays and one short story.

Maryah Converse was a Peace Corps educator in Jordan, 2004-2006, and was studying in Cairo during the 2011 Arab Spring. She has written for publications including *New Madrid Journal, Silk Road Review, The Matador Review, Michigan Quarterly Review*, and *Shooter Literary Magazine*. Maryah holds a Master's in Near Eastern Languages, works in fundraising for refugees, and teaches Arabic in the New York area. She is currently finishing a memoir.

John Michael Flynn's first book of essays, *How The Quiet Breathes*, was published in Spring 2020 by New Meridian Arts. In 2017, he was Writer in Residence at Carl Sandburg's home, Connemara, in North Carolina. Recent poetry collections include *Restless Vanishings*, and *Keepers Meet Questing Eyes* from Leaf Garden press, and three collections of shorts stories, his most recent, *Off To The Next Wherever*, from Fomite Books (www.fomitepress.com). Visit him at www.basilrosa.com.

Debra Frank holds an MFA from Vermont College of Fine Arts. She is delighted to have *The Accident House* included in this collection and is pleased to report that she herself has not been in any car accidents – except for the one caused by a deer's suicidal leap. Debra is writing a memoir about young widowhood and her childhood – when a safe home was not a given. She lives with her partner and her two adult children in Salt Lake City, where she loves to hike and cook. Please visit Debra at debrawilsonfrank.com.

Karin Hedetniemi writes essays about nature, inspiration, and being human. Her creative work and photography appears in *Sky Island Journal, Barren Magazine, Capsule Stories, Door is a Jar Magazine,* and other journals. She won the 2020 nonfiction prize from the Royal City Literary Arts Society. Her home on Vancouver Island, Canada, is filled with travel, gardening, spiritual, and bird books. Her pockets are usually full of sea glass. Karin can be found online at AGoldenHour.com.

Anndee Hochman is a journalist, essayist, storyteller, and teaching artist in Philadelphia. Her column, "The Parent Trip," appears weekly in *The Philadelphia Inquirer;* her work has been published in Poets & Writers, The Jewish Exponent, Broad Street Review, and other venues. She's a four-time Moth Story Slam winner and the author of two books, *Anatomies: A Novella and Stories (not Other Stories)* and *Everyday Acts & Small Subversions: Women Reinventing Family, Community and Home.*

Richard Holinger's poetry, fiction, and essays have appeared in *The Southern Review, Witness, Boulevard,* and elsewhere. He lives an hour west of Chicago in the Fox River Valley. Information regarding his recently published book of poetry, *North of Crivitz,* and his collection of humorous literary essays, *Kangaroo Rabbits and Galvanized Fences,* can be found at richardholinger.net.

Jamie A. Hughes is a writer and editor living in Atlanta, Georgia with her husband, two sons, and a trio of needy cats. Her essays and poetry have been featured in *Barren Magazine, The Bitter Southerner, Ink & Letters, Memoir Mixtape,* and *You Are Here Stories.* You can read more of her work at TousledApostle.com.

Robert Iulo began writing after retiring from a career with the City of New York. His work has appeared in numerous journals and anthologies. He lives in New York City. *The Neighborhood* is a prologue to a memoir that he's writing about growing up in Manhattan's Little Italy.

Kyle Ingrid Johnson writes fiction, nonfiction, and memoir. She won Honorable Mention in the Barry Lopez Prize for Creative Nonfiction published in *Cutthroat.* Her work can be seen in Water ~ Stone, *13th Moon, Welter, OPEN: A Journal of Arts and Letters,* and in the Harvard Bookstore's travel anthology *Around the World.* Kyle Ingrid won First Prize in Madville's *Taboos & Transgressions* anthology, and she has work upcoming in the Quillkeepers Press LGBTQ Anthology. She grew up in Vermont, earned a degree from Vermont College and an MFA in Writing from Goddard. She currently lives in Boston, MA.

Judy Niemi Johnson received her MFA from Augsburg University in 2017. She has written across genres, including fiction, essay, poetry and memoir. Her work often intersects the spiritual and everyday life. She won the John Engman prize for poetry and creative non-fiction and has contributed to the anthology "Naming Hope." She lives in Saint Paul, MN, with her husband.

Deb Liggett is a poet and essayist now making her home in Tucson, Arizona. She and her husband, Jay, met at Grand Canyon, and crossed the nation in varying park assignments – from the Grand Canyon to Big Bend, the Dry Tortugas to Voyageurs, Everglades to Devils Tower, and finally to Alaska. "Marking Our Place" is an essay from her forthcoming memoir, *The Ranger Chronicles: Pilgrim, Paddler, Poet*.

Mel Livatino, during the last decade, has been published multiple times in the following magazines: *The Sewanee Review* (9), *Notre Dame Magazine* (5), *Portland Magazine* (1), *Under the Sun* (11), *Writing on the Edge* (3), and *River Teeth* (1). Eleven of these essays were named Notable Essays of the Year by Robert Atwan's *Best American Essays* annual (2005, 2010, 2011, 2012, 2013, 2014, 2015, 2016, 2017, 2018). This essay was published in the Summer, 2016 issue of *Under the Sun* magazine.

Geoff Martin is a writing coach and editor and currently serves as a CNF contributing editor at *Barren Magazine*. Twice nominated for a Pushcart Prize, his place-based and environmental essays have appeared in *Boulevard*, *The Common*, *Creative Nonfiction*, *The New Quarterly*, and elsewhere. Since drafting "Birdland" in Western

Massachusetts, he has moved twice more: to San Francisco and back to his homeground in Southwestern Ontario with Baby Robin—now a toddler—in tow.

Robert Miltner is the author of two books of poetry, Hotel Utopia (New Rivers Press) and Orpheus & Echo (Etruscan Press); a short story collection, *And Your Bird Can Sing* (Bottom Dog Press); and a collection of creative nonfiction, *Ohio Apertures* (Cornerstone Press, forthcoming 2021). His creative nonfiction has appeared in *Los Angeles Review, McSweeney's* online, *Diagram, Del Sol Review, Kestrel, Great Lakes Review, Hawai'i Pacific Review,* and *Pithead Chapel.*

Vicky Oliver wrote and published six how-to books for the stressed-out career professional under her own name, including *Bad Bosses, Crazy Coworkers and other Office Idiots* (Sourcebooks, 2008). Under her pen name, Diana Forbes, Vicky Oliver also wrote and published a novel titled *Mistress Suffragette* (Penmore Press, 2017). She is a Brown University alumna and is currently enrolled in the MFA program at the New School in Creative Writing.

Lea Page is a member of the Squaw Valley Community of Writers. Her essays have appeared in *The Washington Post, The Rumpus, The Pinch, The Boiler,* and *Entropy,* among others. She is also the author of *Parenting in the Here and Now* (Floris Books, 2015). She lives in rural Montana with her husband and a small circus of semi-domesticated animals. www.LeaPageAuthor.com

Rhonda J. Ray is a retired English professor, specialist in the eighteenth- and early nineteenth-century British literature, and author of a memoir about her childhood spent on a North Carolina tobacco farm. A former writer-editor for public health organizations such as the U.S. Centers for Disease Control and Prevention and other public health agencies, she now devotes her time and interests to writing, rural life, and preservation of her family farm.

Claude Clayton Smith: Professor Emeritus at Ohio Northern University, I am the author of eight books and co-editor/translator of three others. My work has been translated into five languages including Russian and Chinese. I hold a DA from Carnegie-Mellon, an MFA in fiction from the Writers' Workshop at the University of Iowa, an MAT from Yale, and a BA from Wesleyan. For further details, please see my website: claudeclaytonsmith.wordpress.com.

A transplant from Chicago to southern California, **Marsha Lynn Smith** is completing a memoir recalling her time in a rocky romance with a jazz musician and the subsequent father/daughter rift, while juggling single motherhood and working in a surprise career as a Hollywood publicist. She is the recipient of *Longridge Review*'s 2020 Anne C. Barnhill Prize for Creative Nonfiction. Her essays have been published in the *Los Angeles Review of Books*, *River Teeth*, and *Rigorous*. She relishes how time seems to stand still while writing, enjoys reading historical fiction novels, and admits to binge-watching TV dramas set in international locales.

Bill Stifler teaches composition and mythology at Chattanooga State Community College. Originally from southeastern Pennsylvania, he has lived in the Chattanooga area since 1972. He served for several years as a copy editor for *The Academic Exchange* Quarterly and serves as webmaster for the Meacham Writers' Workshop. His work has been published in *Switched-On Gutenberg, Necro Magazine, Verse-Virtual, The Misfit Quill, Fragmented Voices*, and other places.

Elizabeth Templeman lives, writes, and works in the Central-Interior of British Columbia. She has two books of essays, *Notes from the Interior* (Oolichan, 2003), and *Out and Back, Family in Motion* (Atmosphere, June 2021). Individual essays and book reviews have appeared in *The Globe & Mail* ("Facts & Arguments"), and in journals including *CRAFT Literary*, and *Eastern Iowa Review*. You'll find more about her at: elizabethtempleman.trubox.ca.

Elaine Terranova has published nine books of poems, most recently, *Perdido: poems*, which has also been released as an audiobook. Recent poetry and prose has appeared in the *Alaska Quarterly Review, the Laurel Review, Hotel Amerika*, and *Mom Egg Review*. Her awards include the Walt Whitman Award of the Academy of American Poets, the Off the Grid Press Award, a Pushcart Prize, a National Endowment in the Arts Fellowship, and a Pew Fellowship.

Susan Delgado Watts is a native Californian. She is married and has two beautiful daughters. She is Creative Director of her jewelry site Thousand Watt Co. Her writing has appeared in *The Kelp Journal, The Sunlight Press*, and *The San Diego Decameron Anthology Project*. She finds writing to be essential in life.

Lee Zacharias is the author of a collection of short stories, a collection of essays, and 3 novels. Her most recent novel, *Across the Great Lake*, was a 2019 Notable Michigan Book and won the 2020 Philip H. McGath Book Award in Fiction, the 2019 North Carolina Sir Walter Raleigh Award, and a silver medal in literary fiction from the Independent Publishers Association. Her fourth novel, *What a Wonderful World This Could Be*, will be published in June by Madville.

Madelaine Zadik is currently writing a memoir about her relationship with her Aunt Helga, whom she never knew except through letters Helga wrote from prison in Nazi Germany. The essay in this anthology is an excerpt. A longtime horticultural educator at the Botanic Garden of Smith College, she now devotes herself to writing. Her work has appeared in *DoveTales: An International Journal of the Arts, Straw Dog Writers' Guild Pandemic Project, WriteAngles, Public Garden*, and *Roots*.

Editor Biographies

Sam Pickering grew up in Nashville, Tennessee. He spent 67 years in classrooms learning and teaching and has long been a rummager and writer wandering New England and the South, the Mid-East, Britain, Australia, and Canada. He has written some thirty books and is a member of the Fellowship of Southern Writers.

Bob Kunzinger is the author of eight collections of non-fiction and has been widely published in publications such as *World War Two History*, *Southern Humanities Review*, the *Washington Post*, *St. Anthony Messenger*, and more, including notations for essays in *Best American Essays*. He lives and writes in Virginia.

Acknowledgments

- An earlier version of "2 Rms, Family View: The Ones We Call Home," by Anndee Hochman was published in *Purple Clover*; this is a substantially revised and updated version of that essay.
- "4 Generations of Black Hair Matters" by Marsha Lynn Smith was originally published by *Longridge Review* https://longridgereview.com/marsha-lynn-smith/.
- "Becoming Bedouin: Daughter, Teacher, Sister" by Maryah Converse was previously published in *Silk Road Review: a literary crossroads*, Issue 18: The Architecture of Identity, Fall 2017.
- "Going Home Again," by Mel Livatino first appeared in the 2016 issue of *Under the Sun* Magazine.
- "Blue Heaven," by Claude Clayton Smith, appeared in the Spring 2013 issue of *The Mandala Journal*.
- "Marking Our Place" by Deb Liggett was previously published in *Deep Wild: Writing from the Backcountry*, Volume 1, 2019.
- "Not from Around Here," by Bill Stifler, was originally published in 2009 in the online project *The National Gallery of Writing* by the Two Year College Association.
- "On a Rocky Island Coast," by Lee Zacharias was previously published in *27 Views of Greensboro, The Gate City in Prose & Poetry*, Hillsborough, NC: Eno Publishers, 2015.